Priorities of Life

Setting your Priorities Right

ANTHONY BRIGHT ATWAM

authorHouse

Anthony B Atwam

AuthorHouse™ UK
1663 Liberty Drive
Bloomington, IN 47403 USA
www.authorhouse.co.uk
Phone: 0800.197.4150

© 2016 Anthony Bright Atwam. All rights reserved.

No part of this book may be reproduced, stored in a retrieval system, or transmitted by any means without the written permission of the author.

Scripture quotations marked NIV are taken from the Holy Bible, New International Version®. NIV®. Copyright © 1973, 1978, 1984 by International Bible Society. Used by permission of Zondervan. All rights reserved. [Biblica]

Published by AuthorHouse 03/17/2016
ISBN: 978-1-5246-2904-5 (sc)
ISBN: 978-1-5246-2905-2 (hc)
ISBN: 978-1-5246-2903-8 (e)

Print information available on the last page.

Any people depicted in stock imagery provided by Thinkstock are models, and such images are being used for illustrative purposes only.
Certain stock imagery © Thinkstock.

This book is printed on acid-free paper.

Because of the dynamic nature of the Internet, any web addresses or links contained in this book may have changed since publication and may no longer be valid. The views expressed in this work are solely those of the author and do not necessarily reflect the views of the publisher, and the publisher hereby disclaims any responsibility for them.

Dedication & Acknowledgment

It takes special grace to know this God. Those who do not believe in God should give themselves some time to discover Him. I dedicate this book to this Almighty God whom all praise is due.

I appreciate the love and the support from the many wonderful men and women who have served with me in preaching the gospel of Jesus Christ, especially those who proof read the manuscript of this book. Our labour in the Lord will not be in vain. We are going to heaven together! Amen.

Anthony Bright Atwam
(B.Sc, M.Sc, Cert Th, MA)

Table of Contents

Dedication & Acknowledgment 3
1. Introduction 6
   1.1 The book overview 6
   1.2 Importance of Prioritisation 15
2. Guidelines for prioritising your life 18
   2.1 Know the season you are in 18
   2.2 Listening to yourself verses taking in advice 30
   2.3 Procrastination: An enemy of Progress 36
   2.4 Give to Caesar what is Caesar's; Give to God what is God's 40
   2.5 Test everything Hold on to what is good 42
   2.6 The use of our resources 48
   2.7 Life opportunities 49
   2.8 Mistakes some aspirants especially single people make 52
   2.9 Living for Eternity 54
   2.10 Attending to the little foxes that spoils the vine 56
   2.11 Balancing the main thing in your life with other activities ... 57
3. Prioritizing the direction of your Life 61
   3.1 The Case of Naomi: A wrong economic migration 63
   3.2 The lost Son and the joy of returning home 67
   3.3 Discovering the best direction in life 72
      Life guide one: The wide and narrow road of life 72
      Life guide Two: Being led by the Spirit of God 73
      Life guide Three: Making the Kingdom of God a Priority 76

4. Prioritising sacred things & common things 82

    4.1 God is sacred.. 83

    4.2 Certain People are Sacred 85

    4.3 Certain Objects & Places are Sacred...................................... 95

    4.4 Certain Activities are Sacred 103

    4.5 Protecting & respecting the sources of your blessings 106

5. Prioritizing your Spiritual, Social, & Material Capitals 115

    5.1 God is the provider of all Capitals... 117

    5.2 Spiritual Capital 121

    5.3 Social Capital 130

    5.4 Guidelines to build healthy and beneficial relationships 133

    5.5 Material Capital.. 143

    5.6 The unfortunate rejection of God as the source of all capital and its demise 146

6. Some examples of balanced priorities 156

    6.1 The need to prioritize when something is entrusted to you 156

    6.2 The need to prioritise family life, career, and your spirituality .. 162

    6.3 Experiencing a miracle and living the Christian life 164

    6.4 Balancing ministry and family life... 166

    6.5 Worshipping God at home, in the church, & in the public square 168

    6.6 Balanced priority in Christian missions.................................... 177

    6.7 Prioritising what happen at Christian gatherings 180

    6.8 Being born again requires that you shift your priorities............ 183

Consulting Books 186

Chapter 1

Introduction

In today's busy world, many people hardly find time for the most important things in life. But the man or the woman who has learned to prioritise their life will be more productive, less stressful; can have extra time for more important things such as family, friends, career, God, the salvation of the soul, and ultimately make it to heaven after death.

The main aim of this book is to encourage readers to learn to prioritise their lives. This is because in life some things are important than others. God has ordered the world in such a way that some things demand urgent attention while others can wait for a later time. Unfortunately, rather than using less important things to achieve the objectives of more important things, many people major on less important things and minor on more important ones. Scripture tells us this in 1 Corinthians 6:12: 'Everything is permissible but not everything is beneficial. Everything is permissible but I will not be mastered by anything'. In life, some things are good, others too are bad. We have God, Satan is also around. A person reaps what he or she sows. But these are all choices you have to make.

The word 'priority' could be understood in three broad ways. Firstly, it denotes placing one thing as more important than the others in a given situation. The word priority could also mean superiority in rank, position or privilege. And lastly, it could mean the condition of being more important than something or someone else and being dealt with first.

1.1 The book overview

This book is a six chapter volume, with each chapter dealing specifically with one issue. Prioritising things in life has not always been straight forward or easy. In the next chapter, we will look at some guidelines which, if followed can help you to prioritise your life. Some of these guidelines include the following: balancing the main thing with the rest of the other activities, and attending to urgent things first. The others include, knowing the season you are in; spending your resources on important things, as well as keeping what is yours , giving to Caesar what belongs to Caesar, and giving to God what belongs to God (Mark 12:17).

Different seasons demand new life style or attitudes. Therefore understanding the different seasons you are likely to find yourself can be very helpful. For example, there is a time to invest and a time to harvest. Today may not be a good day, but tomorrow can be better. If today is not good, tomorrow will be better; and so you don't have to worry unnecessarily about today if things are not okay; 'each day has enough trouble of its own' (Matthew 6:34). In the case of the farmer, he or she understands that the seed is for sowing, and the sowing is in anticipation of a bountiful harvest. Expecting to harvest when it is the season to invest is missing the dynamics of seasons. You may end up stressing yourself for nothing. One of our duties as humans is to know the right season for everything and making that season a priority while we keep a closer eye on other activities in our lives.

Closely related to this is the question of life opportunities. They come rarely, but when they do, they come to help us change the world around us for better. As Cesar Chavez once said, 'It is possible to become discouraged about the injustice we see everywhere'. But God did not promise us that the world would be humane and just. God gives us the gift of life and allows us to choose the way we will use our limited time and opportunities on earth. When life presents an opportunity to you, this calls for a need to shift your priorities so as to make good use of such opportunity; another typical way of utilising the dynamisms of time and season.

There are things that can wreak havoc to our social, family, and spiritual lives if not attended to. I call this 'attending to the little foxes that spoils the vine'. Examples of these in daily routines may include unreturned calls, un-replied emails, neglecting to wish a loved one anniversary wishes. All these little seemingly unimportant things can wreak havoc if attention is not paid to them. On morality, some of these little foxes are the many subtle common sins that can wreak havoc to our spiritual lives over time. For instance, there are little foxes such as pride, envy, irritability, evil speaking, evil thinking, lying and jealousy. These may have the potential to wreak our lives if not checked. And so you need to spot them out and deal with them as soon as possible. Jesus used strong figurative expression to convey the importance of getting rid of anything that has the potential to rob you of true life:

> If your right eye causes you to sin, gouge it out and throw it away. It is better for you to lose one part of your body than for your whole body to be thrown into hell. And if your right hand causes you to sin, cut it off and throw it away. It is better for you to lose one part of your body than for your whole body to go into hell (Matthew 5:29-30).

When Jesus said get rid of your hand or your eye, He was speaking figuratively. He didn't mean literally to gouge out your eye, because even a blind person can sin. But if that were the only choice, it would be better to go into heaven with one eye or one hand than to go to hell with two. We sometimes tolerate sins in our lives if left unchecked, could eventually destroy us. It is better to experience the pain of removal (getting rid of a bad habit or something we treasure but has the potential to harm us) than to allow the sin to bring judgement and condemnation. Examine your life for anything that causes you to sin, and take every necessary action to avoid it. Jesus is so concerned about people's salvation; He wants everyone to make it to heaven at all cost. Will you go to heaven when you die?

Finally in chapter two of this book, we will look at how living for eternity can help us organise our lives properly. Rick Warren once said, 'living in the light of eternity changes your priorities'. What is eternity? Eternity means to live forever with God on this earth and in heaven. It begins the moment you make Jesus your Lord and saviour by confessing with your mouth and believing in your heart (Romans 10: 8-13). If you factor in the subject of heaven and hell in your dealings, you will focus on those things that can lead you to heaven, thereby prioritizing them over others. In fact, you will be careful about what you do and what you do not do because you know that one day you will give account to God and depending on the verdict on the judgment day, you will either be sentenced to hell or your will be granted access to heaven. The Bible says, 'man is destined to die once, and after that to face judgment' (Hebrews 9:27). People who have a secular view of life do not want to believe that there is heaven or hell. This is a denial of reality; there is heaven, and there is hell.

I am very concern about the growing number of people who are still searching for the ultimate meaning of life. Many people are confused as to what direction of life to take. Some promoters of secularism say human beings are simply high sexed animals who live only for the prestige and pleasures of this life. But can such a narrow view of life guarantee contentment and happiness of life? Can material things alone really satisfy the hunger of the human soul? Will constant care of the body alone satisfy the need of the human spirit? Discovering the purpose or direction of your life can be very liberating. Discovering the right direction in life can help you to use your resources more wisely, be more focused, and can give you a sense of purpose and a peaceful mind. One helpful question could be, where will your present lifestyle lead you to? Chapter three discusses how you can discover and prioritize the direction of your life. It discusses some necessary guidelines and uses examples from the life of two people to demonstrate how life can be very difficult if you find yourself on the wrong side of it. Furthermore, the examples demonstrate how life can also be joyous if you are able to discover the best way to live it. If the direction of one's life is right, he or she will be content and be at peace irrespective of the prevailing circumstances. It is my prayer that as you read through the pages of this book, God will begin to open your eyes to discover the best direction for your life if you are not sure yet.

The lack of material capital can challenge some people to embark on a wrong journey of life. A biblical example that readily comes to mind is the story of a woman called Naomi (Ruth 1-4). In the same way, the abundance of material capital can also challenge some people to embark on a wrong journey of life; of moving them far away from God, their creator like the case of the prodigal son (Luke 15:11-32). A material blessing does not necessarily bring us closer to God; and poverty does not either. What brings us closer to

God is our response to God's grace towards us in any situation we find ourselves. If a rich person will decide to response to God's grace, he or she will be saved. In the same way, if a poor person will decide to response to God's grace he or she will be saved too. To prioritise the direction of your life is a decision that should be based on sound knowledge of what is good and bad; let your decisions be based on absolute truth. Prioritising the purpose or the direction of your life is what chapter three of this book focuses on.

In life some things are special. Some people too have been divinely set apart for specific task in this world. Their purpose is to accomplish specific tasks for the betterment of humanity to the glory of God. When you come across any sacred thing or person, purpose in your heart to give that thing or person a high priority or respect since that very thing or person is meant to be a blessing to you. Many people disrespect or treat the very things or people who are meant to be a blessing to them with contempt to their own detriment. Chapter four draws attention to the sacred world, discussing how to place a priority on things or people who are sacred. The sacred or the supernatural from God point of view could be everything set apart for noble purposes. The chapter also discusses three categories of sacred things and suggest ways of approaching them so that you can benefit from the blessings that come with them.

In chapter five, we discussed Spiritual capital, social capital and material capital as very necessary needs for human survival. Still on the subject of placing priority, spiritual capital should be ranked first, followed by social capital and then material capital. But it is not always easy in practice to prioritize these three capitals. What is spiritual capital? The common definition of what it means to be spiritual in a secular sense is the search for meaning, values, and purpose. But I will go beyond this definition in this book. Here, I define spiritual capital as the strength or the capital we get from the '*spiritus* in order to spend or invest or use. The meaning of *spiritus* (spirit from Latin) is that which gives life or vitality to a system, or a human being. God, the creator of the universe is the ultimate reality of anything spiritual (John 4:23-24); therefore go to this God your creator, if you need true spiritual capital.

Material capital on the other hand, is mainly measured in monetary terms or material terms. Material capital is good, but not good enough to save the human soul from hell. According to the word of God, if you are able to take good care of your material capital, true riches (spiritual capital) can also be added to you as well by the Lord (Luke 16:11). One of the best ways to use your material blessings is to enjoy some and distribute the rest to the needy and come follow Jesus Christ, else it can be a hindrance to your salvation (Luke 18:18-30). 'Food for the stomach and the stomach for food'—but God will destroy them both (1 Corinthians 6:13). Jesus says 'The Spirit [of God] gives life; the flesh counts for nothing. The words I have spoken to you are spirit and they are life' (John 6:63). When God speaks to you and you believe you receive life. When Satan speaks to you and you believe you die spiritually like what happened to the first couple (Genesis 3); unless you later receive life from God. Jesus had to breathe the Spirit of God into the disciples before He could send them to share the gospel: 'Jesus said, Peace be with you! As the Father has sent me, I am sending you. And with that he breathed on them and said, receive the Holy Spirit' (John 20:21-22).

In this book, I have defined social capital as the strength, or the support, or the encouragement, or the love, or the inspiration we can draw from our fellow human beings to enhance our lives in order to achieve our God given potentials. Many at times, the source of the social capital for the individual is often overlooked and much emphasis is placed upon the individual's ability to make contribution to the family, or to the organisation or to the wider society. In the same way, we sometimes mistakenly demand love from people who do not have what it takes to love us. The result of this tendency is that many people are feeling increasingly sapped, depressed, frustrated, and less effective. This is because most of these people do not even know where to turn to in order to be refreshed. In talking about social capital in this book, I am more interested in the source of this capital for the individual to function effectively. Whereas the other definitions I have quoted elsewhere in this book are more directed towards the individual's contribution to a relationship, or an organisation or the wider society. If the individual is okay, he or she can be effective in any situation or role, if he or she wishes to. Carl Jung, the distinguished psychoanalyst who took psychology beyond Freudian view, once said:

> If things go wrong in the world, this is because something is wrong with the individual, because something is wrong with me. Therefore, if I am sensible, I shall put myself right first… in the last analysis, the essential thing is the life of the individual.

Sometimes, we are our own enemies of progress. We sometimes destroy ourselves because of our sinful condition. But if the individual is okay, he or she can be effective in any situation or role if he or she wishes to do so. But how can the individual be okay to make life worth living? One of the time tested ways is for the individual to look beyond him or herself and reach out and make good use of the vast resources available. The average person's experience of life is limited by his or her ego. But there are many resources, spiritual, social, and material available to help the individual to become a better person. The subject of Spiritual capital, social capital and material capital are discussed in details in chapter five of this book.

Many people have lost precious things in life because they could not guard what was entrusted to them. This may be as a result of their inability to take care, or to protect what was entrusted to them. Chapter six looks at some examples of balancing priorities. Everything in life is a gift. Therefore, there is the need to prioritise when something is entrusted to you; being mindful of the people who get close to you; or who you even give your love to. Sometimes it may be necessary that you learn to pray more or change the circles of your friends or acquire new skills when something precious has been entrusted to you.

Chapter six also looks at the subject of worship of God. Worship creates an atmosphere for God's throne to be established in any given situation or place. There are blessings which flow from the throne of God to the people. For example, when Paul and Silas were put in prison for delivering a girl who was suffering from demon possession, prayer and worship brought the presence of God into the prison cell and they were released (Acts 16:25-33). Exodus 23:25-27 tells us further benefits of worshipping God: 'Worship the LORD your God, and his blessing will be on your food and water. I will take away sickness from among you, and none will miscarry or be barren in your land. I will give you a full life span. I will send my terror ahead of you and throw into confusion every nation you encounter. I will make all your enemies turn their backs and run. Please make the worship of God a priority in your life; it is your fundamental duty as a human being. Do you know that refusing to worship the God who created you can incur His wrath? Read the message of the angels:

> Then I saw another angel flying in midair, and he had the eternal gospel to proclaim to those who live on the earth—to every nation, tribe, language and people. He said in a loud voice, Fear God and give him glory, because the hour of his judgment has come. Worship him who made the heavens, the earth, the sea and the springs of water (Revelation 14:6-7).

You have a duty to worship the God who created. In this text, the angels have a duty to tell humanity from every tribe, language, and nation to worship God. Their duty is scheduled for a time yet to come where no human being can safely share the good news about God's salvation. Now, it is the duty of all true worshippers of God to call other people to worship Him; God is reconciling the whole world to himself (2 Corinthians 5:17-21).

This God can be worshipped in the private; in the assemblies of other believers (congregational worship or church worship), and can also be worshipped in the public sphere. Relating this in the order of priority, I will put private worship of God first, followed by worshipping in church, and worshipping God in public sphere in that order. In this book, what I mean by worshipping God in the church is the worship which takes place in a public church building. Genuinely, many people want to worship God at home because they are not able to go out to meet with other people in the church building. Others too think worshipping God at home is the same as worshipping God in the church with other believers. Others too, do not worship God in the church because they do not feel happy about the church environment for various reasons. Others too are of the opinion that some churches extort money from unsuspecting members and some preachers take undue advantage of the ignorance of some members of their congregation so they would not go to church. Regular church attendees also argue that a believer who does not go to church is not a true believer; or if someone is not attending church service regularly that is a sign of backsliding. Attention will be given to some of these issues in chapter six. My view on this subject is that, God expects all true believers to worship Him privately, worship Him in the church, and to worship Him in the public sphere. Jesus' last moment at the garden of Gethsemane (Mount of Olives) explains the importance of private worship, cooperate worship and public worship:

> Jesus went out as usual to the Mount of Olives, and his disciples followed him. On reaching the place, he said to them, "Pray that you will not fall into temptation. He withdrew about a stone's throw beyond them, knelt down and prayed, Father, if you are willing, take this cup from me; yet not my will, but yours be done. An angel from heaven appeared to him and strengthened him (Luke 22:39-43).

In this text, Jesus withdrew about a stone's throw from his disciples to pray alone to God. At that time, that was his private worship (prayer) to God. He needed to draw strength from heaven for the task ahead of him; to suffer injustice at the hands of sinful men, and finally to die alone for the sins of the world. His corporate worship can be seen when he was going to the Mount of Olives with His disciples. It is fine to sing worship songs in public places to honour God. But Jesus' public worship of God came to a climax, lovingly expressed in the death he died on the cross for the sins of the world. When the believer worships God in public, it is possible that he may be admired at times, but like Jesus, the world may end up crucifying you. To quote the former Archbishop of Canterbury's thought on this, he says:

> To be with Jesus is to be where human suffering and pain are found, and it is also to be with other human beings who are invited to be with Jesus. Like the saints before us, we tread a dangerous path- which is also the path to life (**Rowan Williams).**

Jesus says,' whoever serves me must follow me; and where I am, my servant also will be. My Father will honor the one who serves me' (John 12:26).

This book has been written from a fourfold knowledge base:
- My general observations of the world inspired by the Spirit of God, shared with colleagues and friends around the world.
- Ideas and advices from great men and women, past and present.
- My twelve years experience as minister of religion in the Christian church (at the time of writing this book).
- Inspiration from the Holy Scriptures- The Holy Bible.

Sometimes, consciously or unconsciously, we all prioritize things in life. Therefore, I believe knowing the importance of such endeavour can encourage us to cultivate this habit the more.

1.2 Importance of Prioritisation

In this section we will be looking at some of the importance of priority; simply put, why one needs to prioritise one thing over the other.

1. Prioritising creates extra time for life necessities

Many relationships and families have broken down because of lack of quality time together. Several factors could account for this, including, work pressure, financial considerations and also poor planning. Anyone who is able to prioritise things in his or her life will have extra time for other life necessities such as reading, praying, mediation, physical exercise, church attendance, sleeping, socialising, and spending quality time with family members and other love ones.

> I'm starting to judge success by the time I have for myself, the time I spend with family and friends. My priorities are not amending; they are shifting. **Brendan Fraser.**

As Brendan says, one needs to shift their priorities when necessary. Don't just focus on only one thing, but give some attention to other things as well when they become necessary.

2. Prioritising reduces stress

I know that each of us has much to do. Sometimes we feel overwhelmed by the tasks we face. But if we keep our priorities in order, we can accomplish all that we should. We can endure to the end regardless of temptations, problems, and challenges.

> Having my priorities in order has really helped me look better, fresher, and more relaxed, **Kim Cattrall**.

How can stress be reduced by prioritising our lives? There are many causes of stress. Many of life's demands can cause stress, particularly work, relationships and financial problems. Pressure turns into stress when you feel unable to cope. You can only do or handle a few things at a time. So ask yourself, what is it that is most important and urgent? Discover and attend to these first! Prioritising your life can really reduce stress.

3. Prioritising increases productivity

Many people are busy for nothing. They seem to be doing something but have nothing to show for at the end of the day or at the end of their life's journey. This is because they neglect to prioritise their life. Productivity as an economic measure is output per unit input. Inputs include time, labour and capital, while output is typically measured in revenues and other GDP components. Stephen Covey once said:

> The bottom line is, when people are crystal clear about the most important priorities of the organization and the team they work with and prioritise their work around those top priorities, not only are they many times more productive, they discover that they have the time they need to have a whole life.

Productivity is about making profit in whatever you set out to do. Your life must be profitable first to God, your family, yourself, and the wider society. Prioritising your life, hardworking are all ways to become productive.

4. Prioritising can lead to eternal life

On many occasions, Jesus Christ taught the people He met during His earthly ministry, the importance of making eternal life the topmost priority. Jesus told Peter this: 'what good will it be for a man if he gains the whole world, yet forfeits his soul? Or what can a man give in exchange for his soul' (Matthew 16:26). In this text, Jesus had to correct Peter who was one of his followers to make the salvation of his soul his topmost priority. If you gain the whole world, but end up in hell, what have you gained? Thousands of people lose their souls for the most trifling gain, or the most worthless indulgence, nay, often from mere sloth and negligence. Whatever is the object for which men forsake Christ that is the price at which Satan buys their souls. Yet one soul is worth more than all that the world has to offer. This is Christ's judgment upon the matter (Luke 15:10). He knows the price of souls, for he paid for them with his blood on the cross (Revelation 5:9). He will also not underrate the world, for He made it, and love it to redeem it (Colossians 1:1-23). The dying transgressor cannot purchase one hour's respite to seek mercy for his perishing soul. Let us then learn rightly to value our souls, and Christ as the only Saviour of them. Those who prioritise their lives well, not focusing only on their earthly desires, but also listening and obeying what God says, will have eternal life. Such people will respond to the gospel message which invites all people to partake in the blessings of God where those who respond, receive forgiveness of sins, and all the other blessings God has for his creation.

Chapter 2

Guidelines for prioritising your life

In the previous chapter, we looked at some of the benefits of prioritising our lives. In this chapter, we will look at guidelines that can help us in this process. Many people have different things or activities that are really important to them:

> Faith, family, academics, and then sports were the order of priorities in my family. My parents really stuck to these principles when raising me and my two brothers. As long as we took care of everything, they let us play as much basketball as we wanted. **Jeremy Lin**.

The key thing in prioritising your life is to consider carefully what is really important to you in life at any particular time and pursue it while you give a fair attention to the other equally important activities. It is not a wise practice for one to focus on just one particular thing and neglect the rest; a balanced priority is needed. There may be times when we will need to change our priorities because new things are being discovered every day that have the potential of reshaping us. For example, a bachelor or spinster will have to shift his or her priority once they get married. Let us discuss these guidelines further in the following sections.

2.1 Know the season you are in

Another helpful point to be conversant with is to know what season you are in. Life is full of seasons, and this is how God made his world. The good news is that there is a time to be sad and a time to be happy. I personally thank God for the various seasons we have. It is because of the differences in seasons that someone in a sad mood can be hopeful for a brighter morning. 'Weeping, the Bible says, may endure for a night, but joy cometh in the morning' (Psalm 30:5).

Ecclesiastes 3:1-8 summarises some of the main seasons we have on earth:

> There is a time for everything, and a season for every activity under heaven: a time to be born and a time to die, a time to plant and a time to uproot, a time to kill and a time to heal, a time to tear down and a time to build, a time to weep and a time to laugh, a time to mourn and a time to dance, a time to scatter stones and a time to gather them, a time to embrace and a time to refrain, a time to search and a time to give up, a time to keep and a time to throw away, a time to tear and a time to mend, a time to be silent and a time to speak, a time to love and a time to hate, a time for war and a time for peace.

God has arranged everything beautiful under the sun. There is a time and a season for every activity under the sun. The truth is that mankind's happiness to a large extent depends upon doing the will of God in a particular situation. This quotation shows how providence arranges even the smallest concerns. There are certain things mankind cannot alter, so we should endeavour to make the best of things as they are. You cannot change the seasons, but you can easily change your attitude in order to benefit from the season you find yourself. One of our duties as creatures of God is to know the right season for everything and make that season a priority while we keep a closer eye on other activities in our lives.

Different seasons demand new approaches, life styles and attitudes. It is also important to note that, each season comes with its opportunities, challenges and requires its own initiatives. Understanding the phenomena of seasons can help you not to worry too much. For example, when it is time for mourning, mourn; do not complain when in mourning. In times of mourning the bible says 'It is better to go to the house of mourning than to go to the house of feasting, for this is the end of all mankind, and the living will lay it to heart' (Ecclesiastes. 7:2). Do not go to a house of feasting when it is a time of mourning. It is a good practice to take advantage of every opportunity and or situation and learn something new. We can always remind ourselves that, it is a season or a phase, this too shall pass away.

From the scripture alluded to, we noted that there is time limit for the mourning; weeping may endure for a night, but the blessing of the joy endures all day. For those who are mourning, a time of rejoicing is on the way coming. For those in need of spiritual, social or material blessings, a time of abundance is on the way coming. Most of the time we complain when we find ourselves in situations we do not like, but rather than complaining, one helpful question to ask is; what lessons are there for me to learn in this? What season are you in? I pray for a good season to come your way as you read this book in Jesus name.

Someone once said 'when God blesses you, do not unnecessarily raise your standard of living' but raise your standard of your giving alms or donations to the poor; increase your offerings to help preach the gospel of the Kingdom of God. God's blessings in our lives should as a matter of intentional consciousness, benefit other people. In much the same way, changes in weather, comes with its timings and dynamics. Winter season requires that you dress appropriately to keep warm while during the summer, warm clothes are not required. Do the right thing at the right time. Learn to say the right thing at the right time. Know when and where to share your views, and with whom. Many people get into trouble for saying the right words at the wrong time. For example, if you intend to discuss something vital with your boss, do it when he or she is in a good mood. Look for the right time; watch out for the right season!

Closely related is the concept of sowing and harvesting time. For example, it is folly to expect to be harvesting crops when it is time to be sowing. Many people look to harvest when they have not sown. Proverbs 20:4 says 'A sluggard does not plow in season; so at harvest time he looks but finds nothing'. Many people expect promotion when they have not worked hard or remained loyal to their given tasks. If you want promotion, work hard and remain faithful, promotion will come to you at the right time no matter where you are. Proverbs 10:5 says 'He who gathers crops in summer is a wise son, but he who sleeps during harvest is a disgraceful son'. When it is the season to sow, sow your crops, so that when the season of harvest comes, there will be something to hope for. Many people look out for the glory with no preparedness to labour for it. Life has been structured to comprise the two, and as we have noted earlier, there are purposes for the both.

One of the ways to experience the peace and the joys of life is to learn to be honest to oneself and to others around you, and endeavouring to do what is right. Sowing good deeds is one of the ways of doing what is right and there are many ways to sow!

The story is told about a man called Mordecai in the book of Esther. Mordecai was referred to as one of those who 'sat in the king's gate' to indicate his position of closeness to the king. While holding this office, he discovered a plot by the king's chamberlains, Bigthan and Teresh to assassinate the king. Because of Mordecai's vigilance and loyalty to the king, the plot was foiled. His services to the king in this matter were duly recorded in the king's royal diary. The Bible says 'one night the king could not sleep; so he ordered the book of the chronicles (the records of his reign) to be brought in and read to him. It was found in the recordings that Mordecai had exposed Bigthana and Teresh, two of the king's officers who guarded the doorway, and who had conspired to assassinate the King. What reward has been given to Mordecai for this, the King asked (Esther 6:1-3)? In the end, king Ahasuerus Xerxes rewarded Mordecai with a high position in his court for his loyalty. More importantly, Mordecai's own community honored him because he was one who sought the good of his people and one who spoke for the welfare of his whole nation' (Esther 10:3).

There have always been good rewards for people who are unselfish and who take on the good and aspirations of the wider community. Mordecai's family had come to Persia as virtual slaves, captives of Jerusalem's last stand against the Babylonians. Yet even in enemy's territory Mordecai succeeded in his businesses. His relative, Esther, found more success; she was selected from all the beautiful women in the land as King Xerxes' queen.

How could this be possible in the land where Mordecai, Esther, and the Jewish people were slaves serving an autocratic King Xerxes? Esther knew very well the perils of standing up to autocratic Xerxes, she had gotten her job because of the king's furious response to the former queen's brashness (Esther 1:12-2:7). Other historical sources portray Xerxes as a dangerously impulsive king. When a bridge he had ordered to build was destroyed in a storm, he commanded that the sea receive 300 lashes, and then had the bridge builders beheaded. When one of his loyal subjects contributed a huge sum toward a military expedition, Xerxes was so enraptured that he returned the money, along with a handsome gift of his own. But when the same man asked Xerxes to let just one of his sons go free from the draft, Xerxes, enraged, ordered the son cut into two and the army march between the pieces.

But Mordecai and his people found favour with this king and prospered in his kingdom. Scriptures says, 'when a man's ways please the LORD, he makes even his enemies to be at peace with him' (Proverbs, 16:7). When you are diligent in what you do, 'you will stand before kings; you will not stand before just men' (Proverbs, 22:29). Learn to do the right thing at the right time, especially when your service is really needed. The wise man says,'do not withhold good from those to whom it is due, when it is in your power to act' (Proverbs, 3:27).

Returning to the subject of time and seasons, God has said in his word that: 'As long as the earth endures, seedtime and harvest, cold and heat, summer and winter, day and night will never cease (Genesis 8:22). Therefore, sow into your ministry, sow into your education, sow into your spiritual life at the right time. For as long as there is sowing time, the time for harvest will come. Throughout the scriptures, the theme of sowing and reaping has been a recurring one. James 3:18 says 'Peacemakers who sow in peace raise a harvest of righteousness'. Galatians 6:7-10 says 'Do not be deceived: God cannot be mocked. A man reaps what he sows. The one who sows to please his sinful nature, from that nature will reap destruction; the one who sows to please the Spirit, from the Spirit will reap eternal life. Let us not become weary in doing good, for at the proper time we will reap a harvest if we do not give up. Therefore, as we have the opportunity, let us do good to all people, especially to those who belong to the family of believers' (Galatians, 6:8). He who sows sparingly will also reap sparingly, and whoever sows generously will also reap generously' (1 Corinthians 9:6). Those who sow with tears will reap with songs of joy. Those who go out weeping, carrying seed to sow will return with songs of joy, carrying sheaves with them (Psalm, 125:5-6). The above references simply could be the needed assurance and indicative of God's faithfulness concerning time and season. Though it tarries, it pays to wait, for it shall certainly come (Habakkuk 2:3).

The time of God's visitation

Know the season you are in and prioritize your life accordingly. God has different times for visiting people:

> As he approached Jerusalem and saw the city, he wept over it and said, "If you, even you, had only known on this day what would bring you peace—but now it is hidden from your eyes. The days will come upon you when your enemies will build an embankment against you and encircle you and hem you in on every side. They will dash you to the ground, you and the children within your walls. They will not leave one stone on another, because you did not recognize the time of God's coming to you (Luke 19: 41-44).

Jesus' tearful prediction of total destruction of Jerusalem was fulfilled in A.D. 70, when the Romans crushed a Jewish revolt by razing the city. The people did not listen to Jesus' warning. If they did, they would have asked for mercy to be spared of destruction by the Romans. In modern Jerusalem, the 'Wailing Wall' is one of the few places where some of the original stonework of Jerusalem can still be seen. The people in Jerusalem did not recognize the time when God could have told them the impending danger and so they suffered the destruction in A.D 70. In the same way, many people have suffered because they did not heed to God's admonition. They were too busy with other activities and so they missed the time the Lord was talking to them.

But how can we tell the time of God's visitation to us? What should be the appropriate response? We will engage with these questions in the next few paragraphs to raise a pointer to ways we can discern God's visitation and how we should respond to it. Such divine visitations are particularly helpful because there comes a time when no human being can help you except God. God is always at his work, saving, and blessing people through the Gospel of Jesus Christ (John 5:17), and so your time will definitely come. There are many ways God uses to visit us with His blessings. God can use angels to bless you, and He can use the church to bless you. There was a time when St. Peter was sent to Prison. The church waited earnestly on God in prayer for his release. At the end, an angel from heaven was dispatched to help with Peter's release (Acts 12:1-19).

It is God's pleasure to commit his resources to our disposal if we wait on him in prayer. In addition to prayer, it is very beneficial to join a local church and remain faithful there, you will benefit a lot. The pool of believers make us draw strength one from another in times of weakness. As iron the scripture says sharpens iron, so one person sharpens another (Proverbs, 27:17). God can also use fellow human being to bless or communicate his will to you, even a friend or a relative. For example, when you hear a certain message several times in a short space of time, it may be that that very message is for you. The message could come in the form of a dream, or from different people preaching to you or advising you at different times. Acts 3: 26 says 'When God raise up his servant, he sent him first to you to bless you by turning each of you from your wicked ways'.

God can equally use the problems of life as an opportunity to speak to you. Unfortunately, many people try to run away from problems. Life is full of problems. We are therefore called upon by God to solve them with His help. We are commended to run away from sin, but not problems. And in other cases, when a fellow is in problem, we unfortunately, make their cases worse by either avoiding them instead of giving a helping hand. In some cases, we act in a same manner like the friends of Job did. Job, the righteous man who suffered unjustly, once told his friends, 'how long will you torment me and crush me with words' (Job, 19:1-2)? Job's friends were self-acclaimed righteous people who in their attempt to help him out of his problems compounded them through their rather hurting words.

Saul, the first king of Israel is an example of how God can use problems to bless us. Saul was sent by his father to look for a lost donkey. After searching for the lost donkey for days, Saul came back home as an anointed king of Israel (1 Samuel 9-10). In a similar way, David was sent to give food to his brothers who were on battle ground fighting the Philistines. When he saw that his brothers' combat were in trouble, he trusted God for victory and stepped out in faith and fought the enemies and had victory. In the end, David became a king of Israel (1 Samuel 17). The main lesson to be learnt in these two examples is that, we should not run away from problems, but rather we should see problems as opportunities to do something for the betterment of the human race, advancing God's kingdom. Sometimes, do not wait for anyone to tell you to act. I have seen many believers who are not doing anything. They give the excuse that they are waiting to hear from God before they act. It is true that in some situations one has to wait for God's direction, it is also true that in some situations God expects us to act in love to help, especially if we are in a position to do so.

I have met many pastors who give the excuse that they are waiting on God to tell them to plant a church or do missions. But these same pastors will not wait on God to tell them to enrol on a professional course or take up a secular job. Most of the things God want us to do have been written in the Bible for us to obey. Concerning our salvation, the apostle John says 'Jesus performed many other signs in the presence of his disciples that were not recorded. But these are written that we may believe that Jesus is the Messiah, the Son of God, and that by believing, we may have life in his name (John 20:30-31).

Most of the things we need to know, and the solutions to most of our problems, the salvation of our soul, better family life, the way to heaven, how to live the Christian life, how to love God and neighbour etc have been written down in the Bible for us through the inspiration of the Holy Spirit. It is the duty of the church leaders to teach the church members and the wider society the commandments of God, who will also teach others. The apostle Paul advised his spiritual son Timothy:

> You then, my son, be strong in the grace that is in Christ Jesus. And the things you have heard me say in the presence of many witnesses entrust to reliable men who will also be qualified to teach others (2 Timothy 2:1-2).

The numbers of both secular and religious counselors are increasing. But I think we need more teachers of the Bible also. People only go to counselors when they are in trouble or when they need solution to their problems. But teachers of the gospel, with the help and inspiration of God, teach people how they should live their lives. It is better to be taught the best way to live than to go astray before seeking counseling. Many marriages, relationships, and family lives have broken down due to lack of effective teaching. We need more teachers in spiritual things, in morality, in the area of relationships, career, and so on, but equally, we need to learn on our own with the help of God. Read the scripture, read other Holy Spirit inspired books and listen to the gospel message from seasoned people of God. It is the duty of every believer to search and ensure that what he or she is being taught is the truth. St. Paul commended the Berean Christians: 'Now the Berean Jews were of more noble character than those in Thessalonica, for they received the message with great eagerness and examined the Scriptures every day to see if what Paul said was true' (Acts, 17:11). There are many false preaches out there! Sometimes, the right counsel comes in too late. But when the believer knows the word of God and is fully equipped with this divine knowledge, he or she might know the right time to seek counsel.

So far, we have been discussing the various ways God can use to visit you, or speak to you with his blessings. I pray that God uses any means he thinks appropriate to bless you as you read this book. The Bible offers many advices on appropriate responses to God's visitation. Poverty does not necessarily bring us closer to God nor does riches. Seasons of abundance does not bring us closer to God nor do seasons of scarcity. In any situation we find ourselves, what brings us closer to God is our response to the grace of God towards us. Our response to the grace of God is vital to the salvation of our souls. The need for people to believe in what they hear, being hospitable, being humble, showing gratitude, being good listeners and putting into practice what they hear are all appropriate responses to God's divine visitations.

The Holy Spirit says, 'Today, if you hear my voice, do not harden your hearts' (Hebrews 3:7-8). The hardening of the heart is the spring of all other sins. All sins, especially sin committed by God's professing, privileged people, not only provoke God, but it also grieves him. The truth is that we miss a lot of blessings when we hardened our hearts. There are many ways people harden their hearts. Others too feel that they do not need to change their ways, especially the Pharisees in today's church who think they are better than anyone else. These people in the church have 'I know it all attitudes'. They do not humble themselves to be taught the word of God.

There are others too who do not just want to change the way they live for various reasons. There are some too who have decided to live their lives the way they want; they are not opened to any external instructions, they are full of their own opinions; and so they hardened their hearts when they even hear the voice God either audibly or through the pages of scriptures. The wise man in Proverbs 1:8-9 says, 'Listen, my son, to your father's instruction and do not forsake your mother's teaching. They will be a garland to grace your head and a chain to adorn your neck'. Let divine truths and commandments be to us most honourable; let us value them, and then they shall be so to us. This will make thee amiable and honourable in the sight of God and of men, whereas the forsaking of those good counsels will make thee contemptible.

We will now turn to the subject of hospitality. This is one of the responses to God's divine visitation. Hospitality is an important Christian virtue, practice and character that relates, in essence, to the Spirit-enabled ability to show kindness, acceptance and warmth when welcoming guests or strangers. Let us learn to welcome guests, especially strangers, but with caution! Scripture also encourages us in this direction; 'do not forget to show hospitality to strangers, for by so doing some people have shown hospitality to angels without knowing it' (Hebrews 13:2).

The Greek word for "angels" in the Hebrew text above is the same for the word messengers. This in itself would serve to remind us that, though the strangers whom we welcome are only human, they might be special messengers of God. Clement of Rome, in his Epistle to the Corinthians (A.D. 95), appeals to the same examples. The apostle Peter also advises us to 'offer hospitality to one another without grumbling' (1 Peter 4:9). According to Jesus, whoever entertains one of His people, entertains the Lord Himself (Matthew 25:44-45). To be hospitable is good! Please learn to be a nice person to whomever comes your way, not just your friends, you may end up entertaining angels without knowing.

Abraham, in the same manner, through his kindness, hosted angels. At the end, he won the confidence of God and God was able to tell him things that were yet to happen. Abraham saved his brother and family from the destruction that came upon Sodom and Gomorrah as a result of his hospitality (Genesis 18:1-15). In this story, God used the passing by of three sojourners to test Abraham's ability to respond to his visitation, and Abraham understood the time and the season, and he knew exactly what he needed to do. It definitely pays to be hospitable as a believing Christian. On the other hand, in showing hospitality, we need to be cautious because many genuine, sincere, and kind people have been taken advantage of by selfish, insensitive, and ungodly people. The apostle Paul warns us thus:

> In fact, everyone who wants to live a godly life in Christ Jesus will be persecuted, while evil men and impostors will go from bad to worse, deceiving and being deceived (2 Timothy 3:12-13).

There is so much godlessness in these last days to the extent that many people are afraid to be hospitable to strangers. How do we become hospitable to guest and strangers, and at the same time be cautious? To be hospitable means to be generous and friendly in providing what guests and strangers need, and at the same time not compromising your position on your fundamental integrity and values. Do not pretend about it. To be hospitable is rather to create a home where strangers and guests can come and be blessed, not to compromise your personal integrity to satisfy other people's selfish needs.

You can believe all the right things, yet still be dead wrong unless you put into practice what you believe. Do not merely listen to the word [of God] and so deceive yourselves. Do what it says (James 1:22). As already mentioned, putting into practice what God says is one of the best responses to God's divine visitation. There are at times when God will visit you and tell you to do a particular thing. Refusal to do what He tells you is not a helpful way to prioritize your life. God is your Father in heaven. He is the creator of all things, He knows all things and works all things together for the good of his own people (Romans 8:28). The apostle James concludes his discussion on the importance of practicing the word of God by saying that 'anyone who listens to the word but does not do what it says is like a man who looks at his face in a mirror and, after looking at himself, goes away and immediately forgets what he looks like. But the man who looks intently into the perfect law that gives freedom, and continues to do this, not forgetting what he has heard, but doing it—he will be blessed in what he does (James 1:24-25).

I have discussed in detail some benefits of putting God's words into practice in my former book, *Building your Life on the Principles of God: the Solid foundation.*. Let us look at the last appropriate attitude towards God's visitation to be discussed in this book. I will use the account in Luke 17:11-19 about the ten lepers who received healing from Jesus to illustrate the importance of showing gratitude to God when He visits you.

> Now on his way to Jerusalem, Jesus traveled along the border between Samaria and Galilee. As he was going into a village, ten men who had leprosy met him. They stood at a distance and called out in a loud voice, "Jesus, Master, have pity on us! When he saw them, he said, Go, show yourselves to the priests. And as they went, they were cleansed. One of them, when he saw he was healed, came back, praising God in a loud voice. He threw himself at Jesus' feet and thanked him and he was a Samaritan. Jesus asked, "Were not all ten cleansed? Where are the other nine? Was no one found to return and give praise to God except this foreigner? Then he said to him, Rise and go; your faith has made you well.

Christ noticed the one who thus distinguished himself, he was a Samaritan. The others only got the outward cure; he alone got the spiritual blessings. He was made whole. A sense of our spiritual leprosy should make us very humble whenever we draw near to Christ. It is enough to refer ourselves to the compassions of Christ, for they fail not. In this account, only one of those who were healed returned to give thanks. It is expected of us, like him to be very humble in thanksgivings, as well as in prayers.

In John 5:14, Jesus said to a man who had been cured of some illness to stop sinning else something worse may happen to him. When God blesses you, please do not go back to your old way of life. We can take a cue from the story in Matthew 12:43-45:

> When an impure spirit comes out of a person, it goes through arid places seeking rest and does not find it. Then it says, 'I will return to the house I left.' When it arrives, it finds the house unoccupied, swept clean and put in order. ⁴⁵ Then it goes and takes with it seven other spirits more wicked than itself, and they go in and live there. And the final condition of that person is worse than the first.

In relating this story to our discussion on the need to be thankful and grateful, going back to our old way of life after the Lord has blessed us can expose us to a more deadly end. We can also take a cue from St. Peter who said to Jesus: 'Lord, to whom shall we go? You have the words of eternal life' (John 6:68). After many of Jesus' followers had disserted Him, He asked the twelve disciples if they were also going to leave. Peter replied: 'To whom shall we go? Although there are many philosophies and self-styled authorities; Jesus alone has the words of eternal life. People look everywhere for eternal life and miss Christ, the only source of salvation. Stay with Him, even if you are confused or feel lonely.

In this section, we have looked at helpful tips that can guide us to prioritize our lives, and how we can take full advantage of the various seasons of our lives.

2.2 Listening to yourself verses taking in advice

The aim of this section is to help you know when to listen to your instincts or feelings, and when to listen to an advice or instructions from other people, or a source of authority. Sometimes, it is good to listen to yourself, but there are times when it is more beneficial to listen to the advice of other people or an authoritative figure such as a doctor, teacher, Pastor, lawyer etc. Here, let your conscience be your guide. That's good advice only if your conscience does not cheat. There are people whose conscience is seared; they no longer have a pricked conscience even if they do wrong. Allowing a seared conscience to guide you in life is a danger to yourself and other people. Most people find ways to soothe their consciences by rationalizing whatever they want to do. That's why it is best to check with trustworthy people for advice. But beware! Make sure you listen to godly and trusted people's advice not just anybody at all. The devil can send his demons to give you a wrong advice, so beware; don't mistake demons to be the angels of God.

Fortunately or unfortunately, in the Western culture, both self-understanding and socio-cultural arrangements have been developing towards a person-centred direction. In her article, titled *Finding Your Inner*

Cook, Madeleine Bunting writes that 'People are turning inside themselves for answers rather than looking to external religions which people have to fit into'. This is what Paul Heelas and Linda Woodhead termed 'Subjective Turn' in their book, *The Spiritual Revolution*. It is becoming a common practice in Western countries, that people are taking more control over all aspects of their lives rather than letting other people tell them what to do or believe. This subjective turn is quiet courageous, but we need a proper balance here. For example, although a sick patient may know certain things about his or her medical condition, the medical doctor or the nurse who has received extensive training in medical practice certainly knows something the patient does not know, and so the patient needs to listen to the medical doctor in order to receive full and proper treatment. Here, the patient will benefit more if he or she disciplines him or herself, to listen to the instructions from the medical doctor. In education, the student will benefit greatly if he or she listens to the tutor for further guidance. In the same way, humanity will benefit greatly if we will all listen to God, the creator of the universe, who knows all things and who is able to work out all things for our good. Certainly, listening to ourselves is good, but we need to, with great caution, make room for external voices to speak to us.

Let us look at some of the reasons why, sometimes you have to listen to yourself. First, you know yourself better than anyone else does, except God who knew you before you were even born (Jeremiah 1:4-5). In the earthly realm, you have a better understanding of your situation than anyone else, except God. Secondly you are responsible for your own actions, and lastly, God may sometimes tell you something directly, and so listening to someone else can be regarded as an act of disobedience to God.

The narrative in the book of 1 Kings 13 about a young prophet is a classic example of the importance of learning to know when to listen to other people and when not to take in people's advice, except God. In this story, God specifically gave a young prophet some instructions. This young prophet managed to follow the instructions until when he met an old prophet who deceived him into following an advice contrary to what God had told him. Let us read a portion of this narrative:

> So the [old] prophet said to him, Come home with me and eat. The man of God said, "I cannot turn back and go with you, nor can I eat bread or drink water with you in this place. I have been told by the word of the LORD? 'You must not eat bread or drink water there or return by the way you came. The old prophet answered, "I too am a prophet, as you are. And an angel said to me by the word of the LORD? 'Bring him back with you to your house so that he may eat bread and drink water. (But he was lying to him.) So the man of God returned with him and ate and drank in his house. While they were sitting at the table, the word of the LORD came to the old prophet who had brought him back. He cried out to the man of God who had come from Judah, This is what the LORD says: You have defied the word of the LORD and have not kept the command the LORD your God gave you. You came back and ate bread and drank water in the place where he told you not to eat or drink. Therefore your body will not be buried in the tomb of your fathers. When the man of God had finished eating and drinking, the prophet who had brought him back saddled his donkey for him. As he went on his way, a lion met him on the road and killed him, and his body was thrown down on the road, with both the donkey and the lion standing beside it. Some people who passed by saw the body thrown down there, with the lion standing beside the body, and they went and reported it in the city where the old prophet lived. When the old prophet who had brought him back from his journey heard of it, he said, It is the man of God [young prophet] who defied the word of the LORD. The LORD has given him over to the lion, which has mauled him and killed him, as the word of the LORD had warned him (1 Kings 13:15-26).

This is a great lesson to us all. This young prophet should have followed the direct instructions from God instead of listening to a contrary voice from this old prophet. People who go about deceiving people like this old prophet should be very careful. If God has not told you anything, please do not tell people that you have heard from Him. This is an act of wickedness. A wicked person is someone who suppresses the truth (Romans 1:18).

Every wrong doing is sin. But one of the wrong doings which could have immediate and serious consequences in your life is direct disobedience to God's voice. Every human being in this world has a personal responsibility to obey God. When the first couple, Adam and Eve disobeyed God, they were sent out of the beautiful Garden of Eden (Genesis 3). The great prophet Moses was refused entry into the promise land when he disobeyed God by hitting the rock with his staff instead of stretching the staff on the rock as commanded by the Lord (Numbers 20:1-13). Similarly,

Saul, the first king of Israel lost the throne to David when he disobeyed God's instruction (1 Samuel 15). Always seek the face of God concerning every issue, before you give in to any other voice from other people.

It is also true that God can sometimes use experienced or ordinary people to speak to us, but the challenge is, how do you know when to listen to yourself and when to listen to advice from other people. We will look at some helpful guidelines later in this section. But first let us discuss some of the reasons and benefits of cautiously listening to advice from other people. Proverbs 18:2 say *'A fool finds no pleasure in understanding but delights in airing his own opinions'*. Proverbs 19:16 says *'He who obeys instructions guards his life, but he who is contemptuous of his ways will die'*.

Life itself is a gift from God to us and is full of exchanges of giving to others and receiving from others. You give, and also receive advice, love, encouragement, money etc from other people. This is particularly so because no individual is created to be the sole repository of knowledge; you do not know everything. It is therefore important that you learn to receive from others in much the same way as you will be given to others. Secondly, as long as we are still human and living here on earth, we have not yet attained perfection. Therefore, your opinions and how you feel may not be appropriate in all circumstances. Your instinct or feelings can sometimes be wrong. Factors that can contribute to this state of affairs include stress, tiredness or ill-health. In such situations, it is advisable to listen to instructions or receive help from other people, who could advice you on which way to go but with caution. Because no individual is a repository of wisdom, to trust always in one's instincts or feelings, will most likely result in uninformed decision. We may also lose out if God gives us a message through other people. For example, Moses was sent to take the Israelites out of Egypt. God did not speak to the people directly, but to Moses as his servant. The challenge is how to set the balance.

Sometimes, it is wise to keep your opinion to yourself, and listen to advice. In this way, you will have a better understanding of a given situation. Listening to an advice from experienced and wise people with caution has always proved helpful than just airing your opinions. Many men and women have had their lives transformed from glory to glory because they listened to informed advice from other people. I will discuss two Biblical examples of such people: Joshua and Esther. The life of Esther is a good example for the young ladies. But let us look at the life of Joshua first.

Joshua was chosen to be an assistant to Moses, the great prophet who led the nation of Israel from Egypt to the Promised Land. Joshua served under Moses very well without causing trouble to his boss. When the time came for Moses to leave the scene, the mantle of the leadership was passed on to Joshua. God's instruction to Joshua was:

> Do not let this Book of the Law depart from your mouth; meditate on it day and night, so that you may be careful to do everything written in it. Then you will be prosperous and successful (Joshua 1:8).

God was not going to repeat to Joshua what He told Moses. God had already spoken to Moses. Joshua was to follow what Moses told him. I have come across a lot of people who are waiting for God to speak to them directly on issues which God has already told people of old; and are recorded in the Bible. Joshua obeyed these instructions from the Lord, followed what Moses told him, and so he was very successful and he prospered. The life of Joshua is a good model for aspiring leaders. If you serve under someone, please remain faithful and learn to follow instructions. Do not pursue your own agenda. If you do so, you may incur the displeasure of the leader, and consequently, you may forfeit your true blessings.

As already discussed, it is also important that we take advice, especially from more experienced people, and people in higher authority. The life of a young woman called Esther is another classic example of how obedience to authority can positively transform an individual's life. The book of Esther begins with Queen Vashti's refusal to obey a royal order from her husband, King Xerxes. She was subsequently banished, and a search for a new queen began. The king sent out a decree to gather together all the beautiful young women in the empire, and to bring them into the royal harem. Esther was as at this point, a young Jewish lady who accordingly, qualifies to context. In the end, King Xerxes was so pleased with Esther that he made her his queen.

What stood Esther out, which I will encourage young women to imitate, was that, she was opened to advice and was willing to act when necessary. Esther was an orphan raised by her cousin Mordecai (Esther 2). But she listened to, and obeyed every instruction her cousin gave her. When her cousin told her not to disclose her nationality and family background, she obeyed (Esther 2:10). When it was her turn to go to the king, Esther asked for nothing except what Hegai, the eunuch in charge of the royal harem suggested (Esther 2:15). When her cousin Mordecai, asked her for help because she was now the queen, Esther listened to her cousin's plea and offered to help although the task was a risky one (Esther 3). Through the services of Esther and her cousin Mordecai, the people of Israel were saved from Haman's plot to annihilate all the Israelites.

Learning to listen and to follow instructions brings greater blessings to us and other people around us. On the other hand, many great men and women have lost great fortunes, kingdoms, positions of influence, and even their lives because they refused to follow instructions at some point in their lives. I am aware that listening and doing what someone else says is not always easy; one may need to demonstrate humility and sometimes consult others for further advice. We will now turn to guidelines on balancing between listening to yourself and turning to other's for advice.

First, develop your spirituality. 1 Corinthians 2:15 says' The spiritual man [person] makes judgments about all things, but he himself is not subject to any man's judgment'. A spiritual person is someone whose mind is enlightened, and whose heart is renewed by the Spirit of God. Such a person is able to discern all things; he or she is spiritually matured. Hebrews 5:13-14 tells us that 'Anyone who lives on milk, being still an infant, is not acquainted with the teaching about righteousness. But solid food is for the mature, who by constant use have trained themselves to distinguish good from evil. To be able to distinguish good from evil, you have to be spiritually matured. Attaining to a higher state of spiritual maturity can also help you to know when to take in advice and when to listen to yourself. You cannot attain to this level of spiritual alertness on your own. You need help from heaven. Being born again where you receive a new heart and spirit can help you.

You can have your heart renewed by the Spirit of God by asking Him to come into your life and accepting Jesus as your Lord and personal saviour for the forgiveness of your sins (Acts 2:23-40). Don't worry about how it works. The Lord knows the how. Just believe! After receiving this renewal of heart by the Spirit of God, you need to become mature by studying the word of God and through prayers.

We can progress onto spiritual maturity by engaging in spiritual exercises such as prayers, fasting, church attendance, reading the Bible and obeying what it says, worship, abstaining from worldly pleasures, winning souls, giving alms to the poor etc. Ephesians 4:11-16, also provides helpful tips for spiritual growth:

> It was he [Christ], who gave some to be apostles, some to be prophets, some to be evangelists, and some to be pastors and teachers, to prepare God's people for works of service, so that the body of Christ may be built up until we all reach unity in the faith and in the knowledge of the Son of God and become mature, attaining to the whole measure of the fullness of Christ. Then we will no longer be infants, tossed back and forth by the waves, and blown here and there by every wind of teaching and by the cunning and craftiness of men in their deceitful scheming. Instead, speaking the truth in love, we will in all things grow up into him who is the Head, that is, Christ. From him the whole body, joined and held together by every supporting ligament, grows and builds itself up in love, as each part does its work.

In this text, we will notice that Christ has given the church certain people with special grace and task to care for the church members until they become mature. A mature believer is able to know when to go to others for advice, and when to listen to his or herself. Aim to be mature spiritually! Let us look at the next guidelines to help you prioritize your life.

2.3 Procrastination: An enemy of Progress

There is a difference between procrastination and waiting for the right time to do something. We have already discussed in the previous section that there is a time or a season for everything under the sun.

Procrastination is when we keep postponing what can be done now to later dates with no very important reasons. It could also means, to be slow or to delay something that should be done until a later time out of shared laziness. It is common to see people who are in the habit of procrastinating missing out on many blessings and life opportunities.

I consider the act of procrastination as an enemy of progress and a thief of dreams but different people down the history have had different views on the subject of procrastination. Olin Miller once said: 'If you want to make an easy job seem mighty hard, just keep putting off doing it'. Regarding the salvation of the human soul, Edward Irvin once said' procrastination is the kidnapper of souls and the recruiting officer of hell'. People who are not paying attention to the salvation of their soul will miss heaven if they die without being born again. God says in Mark 16: 15-16, 'go into the entire world and preach the good news to all creation. Whoever believes and is baptized will be saved, but whoever does not believe will be condemned'.

Dear reader, have you believed the good news of the kingdom of God? The good news is that, through Jesus Christ people can receive forgiveness of sins leading to the healing and deliverance of their soul, their material provisions is also in the package of believing in Jesus Christ, but most important of all, is the salvation of their soul and eternal life. Are you born again? Have you accepted Jesus Christ as your saviour? Have you asked God to forgive you your sins and to grant you a place in heaven after death? Have you been baptised? Please make these the foremost important things of life.

Please avoid procrastination and attend to vital things in life as early as you can. Time and chance they say wait for no one. It is interesting how sometimes we keep procrastinating important things, but we spend our resources on things which do not move us towards our destiny. Please endeavour to reorder your priorities today. Human beings are created to pass through this life only once. If you have an opportunity to do good, and you can, do not defer or neglect it. Make the best use of every opportunity as we are not sure of what opportunities are there for us tomorrow. For example, the word of God says if you hear his voice today do not hardened your heart.

Why do people procrastinate? Someone once said, 'sometimes if we wait until we are ready, it is possible that we will be waiting for the rest of our lives'. People tend to leave or delay vital things till later days for reasons including the following; laziness, fear, inadequate knowledge, deception from Satan and bad influences. While these could be cogent reasons, they do not explain the possible huge cost of not acting, nor the joy that we would have derived from taking action in time. The logic is to take action at the least opportunity you may have, and sometimes, while in a state of dilemma, it pays to cautiously seek advice. It is usually a blessing to have people who will encourage you to get on to do what will bring blessings to you and to other people.

Sometimes, in crucial moments, a single voice can stir a directionless mass of people to action. Prime Minister Winston Churchill's inspiring oratory may have saved Britain in World War II. American clergyman and civil right leader Martin Luther King's sermons and speeches captured America's conscience in the 1950s and 60s. This is exactly the role the good prophets of God played in the lives of many people, both past and present. The prophet Haggai's message is clear: get your priorities right. Honour God first, a message repeated by Jesus in Matthew 6:33 where he urges everyone to seek the Kingdom of God first and all other things shall be added to them as well. Don't procrastinate; make the kingdom of God a priority.

In the context of what is acceptable worship, the prophet Micah expressed the same concern. In Micah 6:8, he says, God 'has showed you, O man, what is good. And what does the LORD require of you, to act justly and to love mercy and to walk humbly with your God (Micah 6:8). The prophet Malachi gave the same message in the context of giving offertory to God where he urges the people to bring the tithes and the offerings to God's house first. He says, 'Bring the whole tithe into the storehouse, that there may be food in my house. Test me in this, says the LORD Almighty, and see if I will not throw open the floodgates of heaven and pour out so much blessing that you will not have room enough for it. I will prevent pests from devouring your crops, and the vines in your fields will not cast their fruit, says the LORD Almighty' (Malachi 3:10-11). In the same way, the author of this book is encouraging you to set your priorities right, and to put God first, it will amaze you what blessings would come your way.

In the days of the prophet Haggai, the people were not prospering even though they were working very hard. They got it all wrong by focusing and prioritising the wrong things. Haggai's words, similarly, rang clear in a time of confusion. The Jews had come back from their exile in Babylon nearly 20 years before. But they seemed to have forgotten the point of returning. After one false start on the temple, the returned exiles had devoted their energy to building their own houses. The ruins of Solomon's temple stood as a nagging reminder that they had neglected God. Now the prophet Haggai urged these pioneers to 'give careful thought' to their situation. He did not rage like the prophet Jeremiah or build eloquent poems like Isaiah. He put it simply and logically. They had worked hard, but had earned nothing. Their crops were unsuccessful; their earnings disappeared as soon as it comes. Why, Haggai asked? Because they had mistaken their priorities, they needed to put the rebuilding of God temple first.

Let us briefly talk about what made the temple so important to God. After all, the proper sacrifices and rituals could be carried out on a makeshift altar. But God's reputation was at stake. He could not be properly honored so long as the house he called home lay in ruins. The temple symbolized God's presence, and Israel's priorities. Would rebuilding the temple change Israel's financial situation? Returning to the Haggai's story, Haggai's first words promised nothing. He simply said, 'Give careful thought to your ways,' and he pointed out that Israel's lack of prosperity was God's doing. They had worked hard, but God had withheld the rain that their crops needed to grow. A month later Haggai said that God had glorious plans for Israel, plans that would shake the whole earth (Haggai 2:1-9). When we put the things of God first, he blesses us!

The Matthew text we alluded to earlier, states that if we seek God's Kingdom first, He will provide those things that are our needs (Matthew 6:33). As we have said earlier on, in today's hectic and disordered world, believers are admonished to stop making excuses and resisting God's purposes. We are to honour Him by getting on with what he wants us to do.

Please, do not procrastinate, but reorder your priorities. Procrastination can be an enemy of progress if allowed to dictate the pace of your live.

2.4 Give to Caesar what is Caesar's; Give to God what is God's

While in Jerusalem, Jesus was surrounded by hostile groups. The book of Mark chapter twelve, records a series of attempts to bait Jesus: by the Pharisees and Sadducees, by the political Herodians, and by the teachers of the law. Each group challenged Jesus with a situation designed to trap him and to anger the crowd:

> Later they sent some of the Pharisees and Herodians to Jesus to catch him in his words. They came to him and said, Teacher, we know you are a man of integrity. You aren't swayed by men, because you pay no attention to who they are; but you teach the way of God in accordance with the truth. Is it right to pay taxes to Caesar or not? Should we pay or we should not? But Jesus knew their hypocrisy. Why are you trying to trap me? He asked. Bring me a denarius and let me look at it. They brought the coin, and he asked them, Whose portrait is this? And whose inscription?" Caesar's," they replied. Then Jesus said to them, Give to Caesar what belongs to Caesar and to God what is God's. And they were amazed at him (Mark 12:13-17).

Give to Caesar what is Caesar's and to God what is God. Gaius Julius Caesar was a Roman general, statesman, Consul, and notable author of Latin prose. Here, Jesus told the people under Caesar's Jurisdiction to give what belongs to Caesar, and to God what belongs to God. In order of priority, you must give what belongs to God first, keep what is yours, and give what belongs to others. Jesus puts it this way: 'But seek his kingdom first, and these things will be given to you as well (Luke 12:31). Ask heavenly things first and earthly things shall be added to you.

There is abundant evidence of the principle of reciprocity in this world. Learning to give others and learning to receive from others when you need help is good. In Romans 13:7, Paul gave the following advice:

> Give everyone what you owe him: If you owe taxes, pay taxes; if revenue, then revenue; if respect, then respect; if honor, then honor. If you owe someone love, give it to the person. If you owe the government taxes, pay.

Some things belong to God, some for your consumption, and some to other people around you. Do you owe someone love? Please pay your dues by showing the love; do not owe any one anything. The person may be your wife or husband. Again, are you giving to God what is due him? Or you are denying him what is due him, owe no one anything. This is one way of maintaining priority in life, to avoid possible punishment or to avoid hurting someone.

There are two main reasons why you have to give what belongs to God, and what belongs to others to them. As already discussed, such attitude attracts more blessings into your life. In the Old Testament, the first part of the harvest was to be offered to God in gratitude. So when God says, '... I require... the first-fruits and the choicest of your contributions... (Exodus 23:19; Deuteronomy 26)' it means instead of fitting Him into your agenda, you must put Him at the top. He wants your first fruit, not your leftovers. And I think this act is also a sign of respect. One Bible teacher put it like this: 'I've trained myself to start each day by giving God the first-fruits of my time. I've realised that I am not going to get through the day peacefully if I do not. So each morning, I get coffee, and usually while still in my pyjamas, I spend as much time with God as I need to in order to feel I can behave properly and walk in the fruit of the Spirit throughout the day. According to Galatians 5:22, the the fruit of the Spirit is love, joy, peace, patience, kindness, goodness, faithfulness, gentleness and self-control. Seek first His kingdom; seek first to be righteous, and to be in good standing with him, and all other necessary things will be added to you. He is the maker of all things; He has control over all things, and is the provider of all things.

Giving God the first moments of the morning could help keep your priorities right for the rest of the day. A time spent with God has the potential to nourish your soul, and give you strength for the day. The key thing is to seek him first, do not use this gift of time to think about your problems (Matthew, 6:27). Each day comes with its own blessings, troubles, temptation, testing, and times of challenge that is why our prayer need always be Lord, I depend on you for each hour of this day. Let my words, my attitudes, my decision, and my actions bring glory to you.

The second reason why you need to give everyone their due; to God what is due him, to government what is due them, and to other people what you owe them is that for example, if you owe your government taxes, there are legal conditions that might inconvenient you. If you owe a friend or a colleague something and you do not pay, the person may take you to the law court. Jesus advises us this way: 'Settle matters quickly with your adversary who is taking you to court. Do it while you are still with him on the way, or he may hand you over to the judge, and the judge may hand you over to the officer, and you may be thrown into prison. I tell you the truth, you will not get out until you have paid the last penny' (Matthew 5:25-26). 'Give everyone what you owe him: If you owe taxes, pay taxes; if revenue, then revenue; if respect, then respect; if honor, then honor. 'Let no debt remain outstanding, except the continuing debt to love one another, for he who loves his fellowman has fulfilled the law' (Romans 13:7-8).

2.5 Test everything Hold on to what is good

> Test everything. Hold on to the good. Avoid every kind of evil (1 Thessalonians 5:21-22).

In this life, there are good things and there are also things that are not very good. It is your responsibility, and fundamental duty to test everything and hold on to that which is good. Someone may ask what criteria should be used to test what is good. While I will not be able to give a straight forward answer to this question, what I can say here is that we are leaning towards a consumer culture; pick and choose culture and most people make their choices based on their personal preference. Some things may be good, but if it is not what people are looking for, they are rejected.

The way Western society in particular is being structured in which both self-understanding and socio-cultural arrangements have been developing towards a 'person-centred direction', makes defining what is good very difficult; here people are no more interested in absolute truth. This trend has constrained many people to the extent that many people do not look for help outside the narrow reality they have constructed in their own minds. This is one characteristics of postmodernity. 'Absolute claims and universal applications are suspect in postmodernity'. This is because in postmodernity, one of the emphases is on subjective experience and diversity. People are becoming self-centred and will only embrace what will make them feel good.

Unfortunately, because of this trend, many people are not enjoying the vast resources God has made available to humanity. Those who focus on themselves as well as on the Almighty God have at their disposal, vast resources for life. For example, the deistic leaders of the Enlightenment, in so far as they concerned themselves with God, envisaged absolute power above and beyond the world. Our focus in this section is to encourage people to test all things and to hold on to that which is good. The salvation of your soul is good. Securing a good and decent source of income is good. Worshipping God is good. Family life is good. Healthy living is good (3 John 1:2). Loving people and showing kindness is good.

One significant criterion to determine what is good in life is the use of the word of God as a standard. There are other criteria you can use as well, but the word of God is the ultimate because it is the word of God. The book of James 1:17 says, 'Every good and perfect gift is from above, coming down from the Father of the heavenly light'. This should cause us to think about some of these good and perfect gifts from heaven and make every effort to give them a high priority. Although some of these good things are in heaven and are released upon request through prayer.

> God's divine power has given us everything we need for life and godliness through our knowledge of him who called us by his own glory and goodness. Through these he has given us his very great and precious promises, so that through them you may participate in the divine nature and escape the corruption in the world caused by evil desires (2 Peter 1:3-4).

God's divine power has given us everything we need. We can also see this from the creation account in Genesis chapters one and two and also from everyday life. I will mention some of the good things the good Lord has provided for us in a moment, but let us first look at how God, out of deep love and concern looks into our lives and gives us what we really need. May the Lord look into your life and provide you with what you need as you read this book.

Regarding the union of marriage where a man and a woman come together to establish a family, Genesis 2:18 tells us that 'The LORD God said, 'It is not good for the man to be alone. I will make a helper suitable for him'. God himself made the introductions and gave the first couple the delight of each other, body and soul. They also became the first parents, though their very first child (Cain) brought much joy as well as pain (Genesis 4). When the people of Israel needed healing, God sent forth his word and healed their diseases (Psalm 107:20). When the world needed a savior from sin and its consequences, God sent His Son to die for our sins and to reconcile us to himself (Romans 5:6-8; 1 John 4:14). God knows that in this end times, humanity will need spiritual help, and so through the prophet Joel God said: 'I will pour out my Spirit on all people. Your sons and daughters will prophesy, your old men will dream dreams, your young men will see visions. Even on my servants, both men and women, I will pour out my Spirit in those days (Joel 2:28-29). This prophecy was referred to by Peter on the day of Pentecost (Acts 2:17-21). He said it had been fulfilled when the Holy Spirit came on Jesus' disciples. Paul also quoted Joel 2:32 in Romans 10:12-13, making the point that God would respond to Jews and non-Jews without distinction.

Genesis 21:8-21 tells us that when Hagar was sent away with her son Ishmael into the desert, and the water in the skin was gone, she put the boy under one of the bushes. Then she went off and sat down nearby, about a bowshot away. For she thought, I cannot watch the boy die. And as she sat there nearby, she began to sob. God heard the boy crying, and the angel of God called to Hagar from heaven and said to her, what is the matter, Hagar? Do not be afraid; God has heard the boy crying as he lies there. Lift the boy up and take him by the hand, for I will make him into a great nation. Then God opened her eyes and she saw a well of water. So she went and filled the skin with water and gave the boy a drink. God was with the boy as he grew up. He lived in the desert and became an archer' (Genesis 21).

God does not just give us things, but he considers carefully our present needs. In this incident, God provided water for Hagar and her son and blessed the boy. I hope by now you are beginning to see how God provides us with what we really need. He makes a way where there is no way; this is my prayer for you as you read this book.

The following are some of the good and perfect things God has already provided for us. Faith in God is good. If you are going to do anything great in life, there will be opposition, setbacks, delays and critics. When you have big dreams you are going to have big challenges, for these reasons, you will always need to be rest assured of the presence of Him who is greater than he that is in the world– faith is what is needed. Faith in God, the creator of the universe is good (James 1:17; 2 Chronicles 16:9). Many people talk about having faith, but the faith they have is in themselves alone. It is not enough to have faith in yourself because you are limited in power, knowledge, and abilities. Research suggests that no faith in anything other than oneself makes one vulnerable in times of crisis. Jesus says have faith in God (Mark 11:22). Faith is a trust in an object that allows that object to act on your behalf. Faith in God allows God to act on your behalf and this faith we are talking about is a gift from God himself (Ephesians 2:8).

To believe in Jesus Christ as your Lord and saviour is good because it is the believer's only guarantee for eternal life. (1 John 4:14). To be led by the Holy Spirit is good because of the many blessings the Holy Spirits gives to those who will welcome Him into their lives (Galatians 5:25); for as many as are led by the Spirit of God, they are the sons of God (Romans, 8:14). To read the Bible which contains the word of God is very beneficial. It provides us with God's guidance for life and godliness (James 1:25). As already mentioned, to worship God is good. You have a personal duty to worship the God who created you; Revelations 14:6-7 says: 'Then I saw another angel flying in midair, and he had the eternal gospel to proclaim to those who live on the earth—to every nation, tribe, language and people. He said in a loud voice, fear God and give him glory, because the hour of his judgment has come. Worship him who made the heavens, the earth, the sea and the springs of water'.

Therefore, to belong to the church is equally beneficial since the church environment can provide you with a place to worship this great God and a group of other God's children to help you build your spiritual life and to receive more blessings (Matthew 16: 18; Hebrews 12:22-24). Please explore the benefits of testing and holding on to some of the good things I have just mentioned for yourself, you will be glad you did.

One thing you will discover is that most of these good things I have mentioned come from heaven and will go back to heaven. This means that if you also live 'a good life in Christ Jesus' on earth you will also go to heaven after death. God is from heaven and the earth is his footstool (Isaiah 66:1). Jesus Christ the son of God, He is from heaven who came to the earth to show us the way of life; died for our sins; resurrected from death, and went back to heaven, and his is making intercession for those who calls upon him as Lord and saviour (John 6:51; Mark 16:19). The Holy Spirit is from God, the Father in heaven (Romans 8:34). The church is a spiritual family whose citizenship is from heaven (Philippians 3:20), built by Jesus Christ himself, the gates of Hades is unable to prevail against it (Matthew 16:18); the church will be raptured to heaven (1 Thessalonians 4:13–18). All good and perfect things come from above; seek heavenly things in addition to earthly things.

This brings me to the subject of forgiveness. Forgiving other people is good for your health. Receiving forgiveness of sins from God is good for your eternal salvation. Unfortunately, the subject of forgiveness of sins is one of the very important yet neglected subjects in the Christian fraternity today. We need forgiveness so that our guilt can be taken away whenever we sin. Human beings are tripartite being; body, soul, and spirit (1 Thessalonians 5:23). But I must mention here that some people believe we are made up of body and spirit only without a soul. Others too believe the soul and the spirit are the same. But these are theologically debatable issues. The book of 1 Thessalonians 5:23 says 'May God himself, the God of peace, sanctify you through and through. May your whole spirit, soul and body be kept blameless at the coming of our Lord Jesus Christ'. This text tells us that we are made up of body, spirit and soul.

When you sin, the sin defiles your soul and makes it dirty. A dirty soul will make you feel guilty and guilt can make you sorrowful. A dirty soul can make you uncomfortable, it can drive you mad (read Psalm 32). A dirty soul cannot be at peace with God; it cannot relate to Him or make it to heaven unless it is atoned for (Isaiah 59:1-3). A dirty body can be washed with water. Unfortunately there is nothing that can cleanse the human soul except the blood that was shed for that purpose.

In the Old Testament era, the prescription for forgiveness of sins was the blood of animals, on God's altar, as it has been stated; 'For the life of a creature is in the blood, and [God] have given it to you to make atonement for yourselves on the altar' (Leviticus 17:11). It is the blood that makes atonement for our lives. In the New Testament; God has given us his Son Jesus Christ who died on the cross for our sins. There is no need for any animal sacrifice for your sins again (Hebrews 10). Romans 5:6 tell us this: 'You see, just at the right time, when we were still powerless, Christ died for the ungodly'. 'But if we walk in the light, as he is in the light, we have fellowship with one another, and the blood of Jesus, his Son, purifies us from all sin' (1 John 1:7). To receive forgiveness from God is good. Many people are burdened with guilt because of the bad things they have done. Guilt can rob you of happiness and joy. Forgiveness takes away your guilt. I must also mention that forgiveness through the blood of Jesus is a victory over Satan. You can defeat Satan with the blood of Jesus if brings accusations against you (read Revelation 12:7-12). You can also resist Satan if he tries to intimidate you and he will flee from you (James 4:7); by putting on the full armour of God in order to stand against his evil schemes (Ephesians 6:10-18).

Test everything, hold on to that which is good (1 Thessalonians 5:21). As an illustration, Moses' decision to forsake the pleasures of sin and to be identified with the people of God can be considered as an example of how one can hold on to what is good in life (Hebrews 11:24-26). The author of the book of Hebrews launches into a detailed description of faith, complete with references to several dozen biographical models. Some have dubbed Hebrews 11 the 'Faith Hall of Fame'. Hebrews 11:24-26 tells us that by faith Moses, when he had grown up, refused to be known as the son of Pharaoh's daughter. He chose to be mistreated along with the people of God rather than to enjoy the pleasures of sin for a short time. He regarded disgrace for the sake of believing in God as of greater value than the treasures of Egypt, because he was looking ahead to his reward. Surely, Moses earned the good name as one of the faithful servants of God (Hebrews 3:5). Allow yourself to be guided by what is good in life.

In this section, we have been looking at the importance of given a high priority to what is good in life. We have also discussed some good things in life using James 1:17 as our guide: 'Every good and perfect gift is from above, coming down from the Father of the heavenly lights, who does not change like shifting shadows'. Look out for these good things in life and value them.

2.6 The use of our resources

Another measure you can use to prioritise your life is to spend your resources on important things. While the idea of what is important is subjective, and circumstances specific, the Eisenhower Matrix for managing our time can be applied as well. Besides, there is at least, a general consensus on what really matters in life. For example, Proverbs 20:1 say 'Wine is a mocker and beer a brawler; whoever is led astray by them is not wise.' Spending large part of your income and time on such things is most definitely not worth comparing to spending the same on your family. Spending your time and resources to help promote the kingdom of God, missions and other charitable works could as well be more beneficial than spending them on only self-indulgences. Some of the resources you have are 'seeds' which need to be planted for future harvest. Live today for a better future by investing your resources wisely. Many people have destroyed their future at early stage in life out of ignorance, because no one told them they have a good future. Invest your resources wisely

2.7 Life opportunities

According to Bobby Unser, success is where preparation and opportunity meet. When life presents an opportunity to you, this calls for a need to shift priorities so as to make good use of the opportunity coming your way. Opportunity is defined as *a favourable juncture of circumstances or a good chance for advancement or progress*. Opportunity helps us to change the world around us for the better. Our world is not a perfect place yet, if we make good use of the opportunities that come our way, we may advance in life with the help of God to a more humane and just society.

> It is possible to become discouraged about the injustice we see everywhere. But God did not promise us that the world would be humane and just. He gives us the gift of life and allows us to choose the way we will use our limited time on earth. It is an awesome opportunity. Cesar Chavez.

Many people get so worried because of the injustices and the inequalities in this world. But as Cesar Chavez rightly makes his point, God never promised us a just and nice world, he does offer us seasons of opportunities to turn around any undesirable things we see. Even the Lord Jesus, did not paint an-all-splendid picture for us:

> …you are going to have the light just a little while longer. Walk while you have the light, before darkness overtakes you. The man who walks in the dark does not know where he is going. Put your trust in the light while you have it, so that you may become sons of light (John 12:35-36).

Those who are privileged to have received the light of heaven are encouraged to walk as people who are conscious that the light is among or within them; they must shift their priorities to walk in the light. Use your opportunities; do not ask questions to raise objections, but ask questions in order that you may know the truth. The man who thus use the light would not walk in darkness, but would have the light of life (John 8:12). For him that neglects to use the means and faculty he had, both would cease to exist. Light helps us to see clearly, and it helps us to be creative and imaginative.

Do you know that the first thing God called into being during creation was light?

> In the beginning God created the heavens and the earth. Now the earth was formless and empty, darkness was over the surface of the deep, and the Spirit of God was hovering over the waters. And God said, "Let there be light," and there was light. God saw that the light was good, and he separated the light from the darkness (Genesis 1:1-4).

In the same way, the true light from heaven quickens our dark souls to see the glory of Christ. Unfortunately, Satan is preventing many people from experiencing this divine light:

> Satan, who is the god of this world, has blinded the minds of those who do not believe. They are unable to see the glorious light of the Good News. They do not understand this message about the glory of Christ, who is the exact likeness of God (2 Corinthians 4:4).

Satan is using all kinds of means to prevent people from seeing the light of Christ- deception, accusation, and intimidation. He has even planted his agents in churches to cause trouble and pollute people's mind from obeying the word of God. The good news is that, there are many people who are experiencing the light of God's glory. It was this light which enabled Paul of Tarsus, who was once a notorious and blasphemous person, a persecutor of Christians, to become a born again believer, and to advance the cause of the gospel. It is my prayer that you receive this light as you read this book:

> For God, who said, Let light shine out of darkness, made his light shine in our hearts to give us the light of the knowledge of God's glory displayed in the face of Christ' (2 Corinthians 4:6)

For those who want to work in the vineyard of God's kingdom, Jesus has this advice for you:

> As long as it is day, we must do the work of him who sent me. Night is coming, when no one can work. While I am in the world, I am the light of the world (John 9:4).

Jesus is the light of the world. Through him alone, can all people see the light of heaven. The parables of the Hidden Treasure and the Pearl in Matthew 13: 44-46 can be a helpful way to learn to prioritize your lives or shift your priorities once you discover something more valuable in life:

> The kingdom of heaven is like treasure hidden in a field. When a man found it, he hid it again, and then in his joy went and sold all he had and bought that field. Again, the kingdom of heaven is like a merchant looking for fine pearls. When he found one of great value, he went away and sold everything he had and bought it (Matthew 13:44-46).

In this parable, we see both men doing something, shifting their priorities in order to possess the kingdom of God. The first man stumbled into the kingdom of God then he made the kingdom his priority by selling everything he had in order to obtain it. The second man was looking for something precious, but found one more precious than what he was actually looking for; and so went and sold everything he had and bought it.

According to biblical prophecies, this world is coming to an end, for God's kingdom to come (Daniel 2:44; Revelation 11:15). God is building His kingdom. Are you part of it? The kingdom of God is the rule of God in the life of people in this present world, and the world to come. God's kingdom offers many benefits, such as food, peace, joy, forgiveness of sins, and deliverance from evil forces, eternal life, and the gift of the Holy Spirit and so on. To enter the kingdom of God demands repentance (Mark 1:4-5), discipleship to become like Jesus Christ in character, deeds, and service to God, soul winning (Acts 1:8), and making the kingdom of God a priority in life (Matthew 6:33).

In conclusion, we can use the different opportunities presented to us by God as guide in prioritizing our lives. Every opportunity may demand a shift or a re-adjustment of your priorities. 'Make hay while the sun shines'. 'Remember your Creator in the days of your youth, before the days of trouble come and the years approach when you will say, I find no pleasure in them' (Ecclesiastes 12:1).

2.8 Mistakes some aspirants especially single people make

To aspire for something means, having ambition to achieve such a thing. The word 'aspirant 'therefore refers to an individual who has ambition(s) to achieve something. In this section, we will be discussing some of the mistakes aspirants especially single people make in their pursuits of life ambitions.

Inadequate preparation: The fact that you desire or want something in life does not mean you are qualified or you have what it takes to have what you desire. Do not just desire to have it; you must prepare yourself for it as well, else you will be found wanting. Many people make this mistake in many areas of life. For example, someone may aspire to become a manager, yet, he or she fails to work hard, fails to remain faithful or fails to acquire any managerial skills. Acquisition of such skills may include formal education, attending managerial courses and seminars, training under an established manager or reading and watching videos on leadership and management skills. You see, neglecting to perform any of the above and still aspiring to be a manager can be compared to building your castle in the air. The general advice is that you must prepare to receive what you are dreaming to have, else you may be disappointed.

Many single people neglect to prepare themselves to meet the right partner. And so what happens is that, after praying and searching for the dream partner, they become disappointed when their partner finds them unsuitable. Some things in life are for those who have been prepared.

Another mistake single people make is what I call '*am not ready to settle down*' mantra. Time and tide wait for no man or woman. No one is so powerful that they can stop the march of time. If you do not make use of a favourable opportunity, you may never get the same chance again. It is also a mistake for a single man or woman who is looking forward to getting married in the near future to go out with someone they do not intent to marry. Many singles say they are not ready to settle down, and end up missing potential partners. The points and principles discussed in this section can also be considered or applied in other life situations as well.

Two of Jesus' disciples asked him for a favour (Mark 10:35-38). Jesus asked them, what do you want me to do for you? They replied, 'Let one of us sit at your right hand and the other at your left hand in your glory'. Jesus answered them with the following words:

> Jesus said to them, you will drink the cup I drink and be baptized with the baptism I am baptized with, but to sit at my right or left is not for me to grant. These places belong to those for whom they have been prepared (Mark 10:39-40).

The 'throne' says one of old, 'is the prize of toils', not a grace granted to ambition. These guys were ambitious to sit with Jesus in his glory in heaven. Some things are given free of charge, others are not. If you want something, then make it a priority to prepare yourself in order to be qualified for it. Those who want to go to heaven after death or those who want to take part in the rapture at the second coming of Jesus should prepare themselves. 'Dear friends, now we are children of God, and what we will be has not yet been made known. But we know that when he appears, we shall be like him, for we shall see him as he is. Everyone who has this hope in him purifies himself, just as he is pure' (1 John 3:2-3).

The book of Revelation tells us that Jesus Christ is the only worthy one to go to God to receive the future plans of the world written on scrolls sealed with several seals:

> Then I saw in the right hand of him who sat on the throne a scroll with writing on both sides and sealed with seven seals. And I saw a mighty angel proclaiming in a loud voice, "Who is worthy to break the seals and open the scroll? But no one in heaven or on earth or under the earth could open the scroll or even look inside it. I wept and wept because no one was found who was worthy to open the scroll or look inside. Then one of the elders said to me, "Do not weep! See, the Lion of the tribe of Judah, the Root of David, has triumphed. He is able to open the scroll and its seven seals (Revelation 5:1-5).

In life, some things are given to people who have qualified themselves. In this text, Jesus is the only one worthy to open the scroll and the seals. As each seal is broken, more of the scroll can be read to reveal another phase of God's plan for the end of the world.

Certain words and phrases used in the book of Revelation had a clearer meaning to ancient readers familiar with the objects. For example, important documents were sent written on a papyrus scroll sealed with several wax seals. Only the proper person, in the presence of witnesses, could open the document. Thus in this vision, only the "worthy" creature is able to break the seal. This worthy creature is Jesus Christ from the line of King David, the tribe of Judah (Matthew 1:1-17). Entrust your life to Jesus Christ today because He alone knows the future (Revelation 3:10). Jesus eliminated the debt owed by mankind—the debt of sin (John 19:30). He will purchase you for God (Revelation 5:9-10). No one is qualified to represent you before God, only Jesus Christ can!

2. 9 Living for Eternity

One other important guideline to always keep in mind in life is to factor in eternity in everything you do. Rick Warren once said. 'Living in the light of eternity changes your priorities'. Eternity means to live forever with God in heaven. If you factor in heaven or hell in whatever you do, this can help you to prioritize your life well. In fact, you will be careful about what you do and what you do not do, because you know that you will give account to God one day and depending on the verdict, you will either be sentenced to hell or be granted access to heaven: 'man is destined to die once, and after that to face judgment' (Hebrews 9:27).

Jesus says 'Now this is eternal life: that they may know you, the only true God, and Jesus Christ, whom you have sent' (John 17:3). Eternity has to do with your relationship with God on this earth, and the new heaven and earth to come. Those who have eternal life will be in heaven after death. I am looking forward to spending eternal life with God in heaven because I have a relationship with Him through faith in Jesus Christ. I have repented of my sins, been baptised, and am living my life according to the word of God as best as I can with the help of God. Factoring in eternity in everything you do can help you to live a good life, plan well, and stay away from evil behaviour. The Bible says:

> Dear friends, now we are children of God, and what we will be has not yet been made known. But we know that when he appears, we shall be like him, for we shall see him as he is. Everyone who has this hope in him purifies himself, just as he is pure (1 John 3:2-3).

God's children are those who are looking forward to seeing the Lord's second coming; they purify themselves from evil. Another helpful scripture which places emphasis on the importance of factoring in eternity into your life is Luke 12:13-21. Because of the richness of this parable, the entire revelation is quoted:

The Parable of the Rich Fool

> Someone in the crowd said to him, Teacher, tell my brother to divide the inheritance with me. Jesus replied, "Man, who appointed me a judge or an arbiter between you? Then he said to them, Watch out! Be on your guard against all kinds of greed; a man's life does not consist in the abundance of his possessions. And he told them this parable: "The ground of a certain rich man produced a good crop. He thought to himself, 'What shall I do? I have no place to store my crops. Then he said, 'This is what I'll do. I will tear down my barns and build bigger ones, and there I will store all my grain and my goods. And I'll say to myself, You have plenty of good things laid up for many years. Take life easy; eat, drink and be merry. But God said to him, You fool! This very night your life will be taken from you. Then who will get what you have prepared for yourself? This is how it will be with anyone who stores up things for himself but is not rich toward God (Luke 12:13-21).

Money is good only if you prioritise it well, else it can be harmful or it can be a stumbling block to your salvation. In this parable, Jesus refused to get involved in a family dispute about money. Jesus neatly summarized his usual approach to money. He did not condemn the possession of it, but he did warn against putting faith in money to secure the future. The rich man's money did him absolutely no good the night of his death. The lesson is this: trust in God and his kingdom, and free yourself from worry about money and material possessions.

In this parable, the rich man obviously was not very wise; here we have a perfect picture of people whose affections are engrossed in the things of this present life. They forget that riches, honour, and power, are bestowed on them in trust. They do not consider that God has put these things into their hands for the good of others, and for their own improvement in religion and virtue, by the opportunities thus afforded them of exercising holy and benevolent dispositions. When you are blessed with material possessions, keep in mind three things, first spend some on yourself. Second, you have the opportunity to improve your religion by giving some of your possessions to others. Third, always remember that you will be accountable to God one day.

Many people do not know what God expects from recipients of divine blessings, and so they rather look upon these advantages as instruments of self-indulgence and luxury, and use them unwisely. But at the very time when they are inwardly applauding themselves, in having such an abundance of the means of pleasure, and are laying schemes for futurity, as if they were never to die, and are thinking of nothing but happy days, God suddenly strips them of all their joy. People who are not rich towards God may suffer sudden tragedy including possible death, like the rich man who did not consider serving God or helping the needy as a priority in his life. What good will it be for a man, if he gains the whole world, yet forfeits his soul in condemnation? Or what can a man give in exchange for his soul (Matthew, 16:26)?

In this chapter, we have been looking at some of the guidelines that can help in prioritising our lives. Some of these are balancing the main thing with the rest of the other activities, attending to urgent things first, Knowing the season you are in, Spend your resources on important things, Giving to Caesar what belongs to Caesar, and to God, what belong to him, and Living for Eternity. Let us discuss the next guidelines in the next section.

2.10 Attending to the little foxes that spoils the vine

There are some unimportant things that can wreak havoc to our social, family and spiritual lives if not attended to. King Solomon calls these the little foxes:

> Catch for us the foxes, the little foxes that ruin the vineyards,
> our vineyards that are in bloom (Song of Songs 2:15).

These little foxes creep in subtly and start to nibble away when they realize the vines are unattended and nobody is watching them. These little seemingly unimportant things, if not attended to can have devastating consequences; can wreak havoc to your social, spiritual, and family lives. The best way to deal with these foxes is to attend to them, do not neglect them. Don't think they are not important, they are. You can for example, use some of your hobby time to reply emails, return some calls, read your Bible, or spend some time in meditation.

The Songs of Solomon referred to form one of the poetical books of the Bible. It is a love story and a wonderful picture of the relationship between Christ and the church. 'The Shunammite was driven into the vineyard by her brothers to care for the vines. The first grapes had blossomed on the vines. Her responsibility was to care for and watch the tender grapes. However, as she watched the tender new grapes, she saw that there were little foxes who also took notice of these grapes. They watched to see when the opportunity could arise for them to slyly start nibbling away at the grapes. Allegorical interpretations make these foxes symbolize 'false teachers' in the church (compare Ezekiel 13:4). Just as a vine that has been chewed up by little foxes loses its value and fruit-bearing ability, a Christian who allows the little foxes to nibble away his or her productivity and his spiritual life becomes useless and barren with time. Please, learn to deal with any issue which has the potential to destroy your life.

2.11 Balancing the main thing in your life with other activities

The last guideline to be discussed in this book for setting your priorities right is to learn to balance the main thing with the rest of other activities in your life.

The story is told of Bob Pierce, who founded the well-known Christian relief organization, World Vision. He was a successful evangelist, seeing thousands make professions of faith in Christ at crusades in the Far East. He was highly respected in the Christian circles as a great leader. He raised millions to help the needy in Asia. And yet, it was reported that he was unable to balance his family life with his ministry. The enemy is always after God's servants to harm them, especially if given the slightest opportunity. Unfortunately, one of this great man's daughters committed suicide. He and his wife eventually got divorced, and World Vision, the organization he founded, had to fire him because of his explosive temper and his inability to work well with others. He was very successful at the main thing God told him to do, but he did not balance the main thing with the rest of the other things in his life- namely family and his own character.

Like everyone else, every minister of the gospel has a personal responsibility to make sure he or she is transformed into the character of Christ. Probably this man did not work on his character enough. Regarding the death of his daughter, we do not know why the daughter committed suicide, but the fact that he was a powerful servant of God did not mean his children were exempted from life challenges. Each person must seek the help of God for him or herself. There are many sources of help available to us all. People who commit suicide for example, are great men and women who unfortunately at the lowest point of their lives did not seek help, but decided to take their suicidal thoughts to its logical conclusion. Please learn to seek help when you are in crisis and humbly accept the help that will be given. With the help of the Lord, all will be well in Jesus name.

This great minister's daughter took her own life. Many people like this minister have done the same thing: succeeding in their careers, only to fail at home. Some have built hugely successful ministries, political life, and businesses only to succumb to pride or immorality. Immorality and pride can turn even an angel into devil. Sadly, many people do not see immoral lifestyle and pride as a treat to their very lives. Even in less dramatic ways, it is easy to get into a battle over some minor issue and forget the cause of the main thing at stake. In family context, a wife should be godly, and should be able to prioritize her life in order to have enough time for God, herself, her family, and her career. In the same way, the husband should lead the family with God's covering, loving the wife and setting the correct path for the future of the children. Let us briefly look at the subject of truth, a treasure being thrown away by many people today!

Let the truth stand out in any given situation! Speak the truth using an appropriate approach. To make the other person feel good by polishing or concealing the truth can be downright harmful. This is called flattery. Flattery can leave a trusting friend unprepared for troubles ahead. Proverbs 28:23 says, 'Whoever flatters his neighbor is spreading a net for his feet.' Instead of been economical with the truth to a friend, we have the obligation to warn a friend gently where he or she is heading. 'He who rebukes a person will in the end gain more favor than he who has a flattering tongues' says Proverbs 28:23.

We need a balanced message from the church pulpit. Church leaders, communities leaders and people in authority who are called upon to serve people should endeavor to speak the truth in love to the people they serve even if it seems difficult to do so. Both the prophet Jeremiah and Ezekiel condemned leaders who flatter the people for personal gain:

> From the least to the greatest, all are greedy for gain; prophets and priests alike, all practice deceit. They dress the wound of my people as though it were not serious. 'Peace, peace,' they say, when there is no peace (Jeremiah 6:13-14).

A good medical doctor sometimes has to convey bad tidings, delivering the report on diagnosis of cancer, for example so the right treatment can be administered early. But in the land of Judah just us it is becoming common in our days, the spiritual "doctors" (prophets and priests) only gave out sweet news to their itching listeners. They covered up serious wounds with a Band-aid. 'They have seduced my people', says the Lord, - they have caused God's people to err, both with respect to the greatness of their own guilt, and my displeasure on account of it, as if both were less than they really are, and no great danger was to be apprehended. They deceived them, by assuring them that none of those judgments should overtake them which Jeremiah and the other true prophets threatened them with, and they spoke peace to men's consciences upon false grounds and principles. Thus they obstructed and drew them out of the way of repentance, and reformation into which the other prophets were endeavouring to bring them.

The most dangerous seducers are those who suggest to sinners things which tends to lessen their dread of sin, or their fear of God. The apostle Paul warns in a similarly way:

> In the presence of God and of Christ Jesus, who will judge the living and the dead, and in view of his appearing and his kingdom, I give you this charge: Preach the Word; be prepared in season and out of season; correct, rebuke and encourage—with great patience and careful instruction. For the time will come when men will not put up with sound doctrine. Instead, to suit their own desires, they will gather around them a great number of teachers to say what their itching ears want to hear. They will turn their ears away from the truth and turn aside to myths (2 Timothy 4:1-4).

The society needs preachers who preach the true Word of God in season and out of season; correcting, rebuking and encouraging, with great patience and careful instruction. Many preachers these days only preach and teach inspirational messages. They have neglected the message of repentance from sin and worldliness. Preachers who are not telling their listeners to turn from sin are very close to becoming false preachers, if they are not one already. Repentance is a core component of the gospel of the kingdom of God:

> After John was put in prison; Jesus went into Galilee, proclaiming the good news of God. The time has come, "he said. The kingdom of God is near. Repent and believe the good news! (Mark 1:14-15).

Following Jesus' footpath, he healed the sick, fed the people, forgave their sins, encouraged people, but he also preached repentance from sin, and so should every true minister of the gospel. The core principle discussed in this section is to look out for the weightier matters in life and give due attention to them.

We shall continue our discussion on the subject of priority in the next chapter.

Chapter 3

Prioritizing the direction of your Life

Where is your life heading to? Discovering the right direction for your life can be helpful in many ways; it can help you to spend your resources on the right things, be wiser, more focused in life, as well as giving you a sense of purpose and a peaceful mind. Someone said this about discovering life's direction:

> I used to spend so much time reacting and responding to everyone else that my life had no direction. Other people's lives, problems, and wants set the course for my life. Once I realized it was okay for me to think about and identify what I wanted, remarkable things began to take place in my life.

Many people are confused about what course to direct their life. There are two main reasons why some people are not discovering the best direction for their lives. First, lack of the right knowledge, and secondly lack of willingness to be on the right path of life. Take your time to discover where God has placed you in His creation. Take a look at how the various parts of the human body have been arranged and fitted together. Every part of the human body plays a unique and vital role. The hand cannot function well if it tries to take the position and the role of the leg. In the same way, many people are not at their best because they have abandoned their position and role in this world. Some people too are roaming aimlessly. Jesus Christ who is the way, the truth, and the life can help you to discover the best direction for your life, and also help you to build the spiritual faith you need to be on such a journey. If the direction of your life is right, you will find contentment, and be at peace irrespective of prevailing circumstances.

In this chapter, we will look at some of the guidelines that are helpful in the journey of discovering the best direction of life. We will draw examples from the life of two individuals who, for lack of a balanced priority, both had it all wrong. Like many people in today's world, the story of Naomi and the parable of the prodigal son are classic examples of how people can easily wreck their lives as they journey on the wrong path of life. Naomi had left Israel for Moab, married, and secured, but she returned widowed and poor. Her return to her homeland however, gave her the opportunity to remedy the remaining parts of her life. It is never too late to start again. In the same manner, the prodigal son left the father with his portion of the father's massive wealth. Out of mismanagement, and lack of proper direction, he became poor, destitute, and needy. Upon realising his folly, coming back to his senses, and repenting of his actions, he was restored back to his father. These two stories and the character in them are practical indications that, human beings in their nature are without perfection. Also, there is a true understanding of how the compassion of God is available to people who have gone astray.

The two stories aforementioned present a dialectical approach to life journeys. On the one hand, the lack of material capital can challenge people to embark on the wrong course of life as was the case of Naomi. On the other hand, the abundance of material capital can also challenge some people to embark on a wrong journey of life; moving them away from God, their creator as was the case of the prodigal son. Scarcity can cause people to make wrong decisions; material abundance can also cause people to make wrong decisions. How you response to any situation you find yourself is a key determinant of how far you will go.

Any decision or lifestyle that will cause you to draw closer to God is certainly a good decision, although it takes time for people to see their need for God. You will never regret it, for knowing God relationally. At the same time, any decision or lifestyles that will move you farther away from God is not a good one to follow through.

Someone once said; a journey of thousand miles begins with one step. While there might be significant truth in such saying, there is a question yet unanswered- in what direction should we take the first step? I am compelled to argue that sometimes it is better to take no step at all than to take thousand steps towards the wrong direction. Many of us may appear as knowing what we really want to do in life, and what we hope to achieve with that which we want to do. Sadly, many of these people are on the wrong path. It can be a waste of time in life to be on the path leading to the wrong destination. Do you know that it is not a wise thing to invest in someone who is on the wrong path towards the wrong destination? That is why God always waits until people return and turn to him before He grants them certain blessings. Some people started life on the right path, but somehow they made the wrong turn and so they end up wandering in life aimlessly wasting their fuel on the wrong road. In life, the moment you turn to the wrong path, the divine grace on you begins to dwindle, the light of the divine begins to dim, your spiritual strength begins to wade, and the result is that you will become a wanderer, lost, poor and destitute unless there is a change of action.

Whatever your situation is, it is my prayer that before you finish reading this chapter you will discover the right path to journey on. The lost sheep was found; the exiled son perishing with hunger came back to his father's house. It is my prayer that in case you have lost your way in life, the good Lord will bring you back onto the path of righteousness for his name sake, amen.

3.1 The Case of Naomi: A wrong economic migration

A man called Elimelech, his wife Naomi, and their two sons, Mahlon and Kilion, migrated from Bethlehem to settle in Moab because there was a severe famine in Bethlehem. Unfortunately, Naomi's husband and her two sons died in Moab. Naomi had left Israel married and secured, but she returned widowed and poor until the Lord blessed her again upon her returned to Israel (Ruth 1-4).

The journey from Bethlehem to settle in Moab was a wrong economic migration. It was a wrong journey for Naomi in many ways. First, Naomi and her family left Israel at a time when the nation was in economic crisis, probably due to Israel's disobedience to God. But the solution was not to run away, but to seek collective forgiveness from the Lord. In the book of Deuteronomy, the Lord had forewarned Israel that, the nation will suffer calamity, famine, and invasion by their enemies if they refuse to obey his commandments (Deuteronomy, 28:15-68). This seems to be exactly what happened in Israel at the time Naomi left her hometown to Moab. It was similar to the days when the Babylonian kingdom led by King Nebuchadnezzar invaded Israel because of disobedience. Some people were planning to migrate to Egypt to escape captivity. But God sent his prophet to tell them, not to do so because even if they run to another country the same calamity will follow them. The only solution to their crisis was repentance (Jeremiah 42:13-22).

Perhaps, Naomi thought by migrating to another country, she and her family would escape the hardship in Israel because of the nation's disobedience. But probably she forgot that migrating to another country was not the solution to the problem because God had said that, whether they come in or they go out they will be disciplined once they disobey him, unless they change their ways for good (Deuteronomy 28:19). And truly Naomi was not blessed when she left her country to another country for economic reasons. It is a terrible thing for a person to think he or she can run away from the protective arms of God. Instead of running, it might be more helpful to take a reflective look at approaching prevailing circumstances in the fear and counsel of God. Please do not run if there is something you must do to remedy the situation.

Sometimes we simply need to repent of our ways. Many people keep changing jobs instead of taking their time to change themselves. Some also keep on changing partners instead of changing their attitudes to become better persons. If Naomi and her family had stayed to seek the face of God for mercy, they probably might not have experienced such a great catastrophe.

Secondly, the reason why Naomi's migration to Moab was a wrong economic move is because at that time, there were many curses on that country, Moab. Genesis 19:30-38 tells us that the Moabites were descendants of Lot. Lot's wife had become a pillar of salt when she disobeyed the angel's commandment not to look back at the destruction of Sodom and Gomorrah (Genesis 19:26). When Lot and his two daughters finally settled in the mountains, there were no men there to marry his daughters to reproduce. So the daughters got their father drunk and slept with him, one after another. One of the children from that 'one night adventure' was a man called Moab whose descendants became known as the Moabites (Genesis 19:30-38).

In the Old Testament days, 'no one born of a forbidden marriage or any of his descendants may enter the assembly of the LORD, even down to the tenth generation' unless they seek forgiveness of sins from the Lord (Deuteronomy 23:2); but under the New Testament covenant in Christ Jesus the situation has changed; everyone is welcome to the Lord's presence to receive forgiveness of sins. This is the reason Jesus ate with sinners (Luke 5:30), although He did not take part in their sins but urged them to repent for the Kingdom of God is at hand (Mark 1:14-15). Everyone is a sinner, and is in need of forgiveness: 'for all have sinned and fall short of the glory of God, and are justified freely by his grace through the redemption that came by Christ Jesus' (Romans 3:23-24).

So according to the law of the Israelites, the Moabites were not supposed to enter into the assembly of the Lord. The question is, how can a child of God be blessed in a country which is forbidden to enter into the assembly of the Lord, without repentance? This brings back the point earlier made that we need to endeavor to be knowledgeable enough about prevailing circumstances. Naomi and her family should have known their history very well.

Further to this, while Israel sojourned from Egypt to Canaan, the Moabites acted with a great deal of inhumanity. They opposed the Israelites, and refused them passage[1] through their land. And though God spared them from the conquest, He excluded the Moabites and their seed, even to the tenth generation from the peculiar privileges of his people. Later Moses, the servant of the Lord recorded and mentioned this to their hearings: 'No

---

[1] See Numbers 22:1-24:25

Ammonite or Moabite or any of their descendants may enter the assembly of the LORD. For they did not come to meet you [the Israelites] with bread and water on your way when you came out of Egypt, and they hired Balaam son of Beor from Pethor in Aram Naharaim to pronounce a curse on you"[2].

The Moabites were forbidden from worshiping God, unless perhaps they ask for forgiveness. It is a terrible thing to be expelled from the presence of God. David said to God, you can take everything (including the throne) from me, except your presence (Psalms 51). To be expelled from the presence of God could be compared to the experience of hell, since hell itself is eternal separation from God. This is what Cain said when God expelled him from His presence for killing his brother Abel:

> Cain said to the LORD, "My punishment is more than I can bear. Today you are driving me from the land, and I will be hidden from your presence; I will be a restless wanderer on the earth, and whoever finds me will kill me (Genesis 4:13-14).

So if, the Moabites were not to enter the Assembly of God, then it means there was no divine blessing in the country for a foreigner like Naomi to benefit from, unless of course she herself was a blessed person. Naomi and her family were themselves running from catastrophe from their country because of possible disobedience to God. So they were not innocent either. This is more like the idiomatic expression; 'from frying pan to fire'. When you are going through difficult times, it is wise to seek refuge where you can receive mercy and grace from God. The book of Hebrews advises us thus:

> Therefore, since we have a great high priest who has gone through the heavens, Jesus the Son of God, let us hold firmly to the faith we profess. For we do not have a high priest who is unable to sympathize with our weaknesses, but we have one who has been tempted in every way, just as we are—yet was without sin. Let us then approach the throne of grace with confidence, so that we may receive mercy and find grace to help us in our time of need (Hebrews 4:14-16).

---

[2] Deuteronomy 23:3-4

Jesus Christ is the Great High Priest who had passed through the heavens. As the high priest passed through the Holy Place to enter the Holy of Holies in the Old Testament, in the New Testament Jesus 'ascended up far above all heavens,' and sat at the right hand of God and making intercession on behalf of all those who will call upon him. Before his ascension, Jesus told his disciples: 'You may ask me for anything in my name, and I will do it' (John 14:14). Let us return to our discussion on the third reason why Naomi's migration to the country of the Moabites was a wrong economic journey. Where is your life heading to?

The third reason is that the Moabites were also gross idolaters, worshipping Chemosh and Baalpeor with obscene rites (Numbers 25:1-18; 2 Kings 3:27). From these historical data, it is not difficult for one to conclude that the Moabites were a cursed people at the time Naomi and her family were migrating to settle there, a possible reason why she lost everything. It would have been safer for Naomi and her family to have stayed in Israel to experience the famine alongside with the people of God. Naomi made a wrong choice, and so she suffered for her wrong choice accordingly. We will always account for our actions, good or bad.

The good news however is that, there is always a blessing after returning to the Lord! Both Naomi and Ruth her daughter-in law went back to Israel, to worship the Lord and so they were blessed. Naomi was comforted and Ruth who had lost the husband in her country Moab, had an opportunity to remarry a man of good standing in Israel, and so she had a family of her own (Ruth 1-4). I pray that as you read this book, the gracious God will restore to you all that you have lost in life and place you on a path of righteousness for his name sake. Be blessed as you read this book.

3.2 The lost Son and the joy of returning home

We have seen in the previous section that poverty or a lack of material capital can challenge some people to embark on a wrong journey in life. In this section, we will see how the abundance of material capital can also challenge people to embark on a wrong journey of life, moving them far away from God, their creator. The story of the prodigal son[3] recorded in Luke 15:11-32 could be regarded a summary of God's message to the world. The *Prodigal Son*, also known the *Lost Son*, is one of the parables of Jesus, and it appears only in one of the gospels of the New Testament, the book of Luke.

According to the Gospel of Luke (Luke 15:11-32), a father gives his younger son his share of inheritance because the son unethically demanded for it. The younger son, left home, and went to a far country. After wasting all his fortunes on extravagant lifestyle, he became hungry when a famine broke out on the land. Unable to bear the suffering, he then returns home to his father with the hope of begging to be employed as a servant. Regardless, the father finds him on the road and immediately welcomes him back as his son and holds a feast to celebrate his return. The older son refuses to participate, arguing that all the time he has been working for the father; he has not been given the recognition they were giving his recalcitrant brother. The father reminds the older son that everything he, the father has belongs to the older son's (his inheritance) but that they should still celebrate the return of the younger son, because he was lost and is now found.

Although the text is somehow lengthy, it is helpful to quote it in full.
There was a man who had two sons. The younger one said to his father, Father; give me my share of the estate. So he divided his property between them. Not long after that, the younger son got together all he had, set off for a distant country and there squandered his wealth in wild living. After he had spent everything, there was a severe famine in that whole country, and he began to be in need. So he went and hired himself out to a citizen of that country, who sent him to his fields to feed pigs. He longed to fill his stomach with the pods that the pigs were eating, but no one gave him anything. When he came to his senses, he said, 'How many of my father's hired men have food to spare, and here I am starving to death! I will set out and go back to my father and say to him: Father, I have sinned against heaven and against you. I am no longer worthy to be called your son; make me like one of your hired men. So he got up and went to his father. But while he was still a long way off, his father saw him and was filled with compassion for him; he ran to his son, threw his arms around him and kissed him. The son said to him, 'Father, I

---
[3] The word 'prodigal' means 'wastefully extravagant'

have sinned against heaven and against you. I am no longer worthy to be called your son. But the father said to his servants, Quick! Bring the best robe and put it on him. Put a ring on his finger and sandals on his feet. Bring the fattened calf and kill it. Let's have a feast and celebrate. For this son of mine was dead and is alive again; he was lost and is found. So they began to celebrate. Meanwhile, the older son was in the field. When he came near the house, he heard music and dancing. So he called one of the servants and asked him what was going on. 'Your brother has come, he replied, and your father has killed the fattened calf because he has him back safe and sound. The older brother became angry and refused to go in. So his father went out and pleaded with him. But he answered his father, 'Look! All these years I have been slaving for you and never disobeyed your orders. Yet you never gave me even a young goat so I could celebrate with my friends. But when this son of yours who has squandered your property with prostitutes comes home, you kill the fattened calf for him! 'My son, the father said, you are always with me, and everything I have is yours. But we had to celebrate and be glad, because this brother of yours was dead and is alive again; he was lost and is found (Luke 15:11-32).

There are a lot of lessons we can learn from this story.

The freedom of choice- the younger son decided to go away but, the older son decided to serve at home; the father respected their decisions. In the same way, everyone has the choice to stay with God and serve Him in His kingdom or go away refusing to serve him.

The consequences of our choices- in the same way, whatever choice we make, we are liable to face its consequences. It is a dangerous thing to move away from God; our safest place in this turbulent and world of uncertainty is with the Lord. Like the prodigal son, if you move away from God, you are likely to end up like him. He was simply out of reach of his father. People, who do not have a relationship with God, are out of reach with him. Staying at home with your God is the same as being in his house (church). David said in Psalm 122:1, 'I was glad when they said unto me, let us go into the house of the LORD'.

What true repentance is- the prodigal son asked for forgiveness of sin, and showed the willingness to stay to serve the father. This is what true repentance should be. Many people come to God because of what God is able to give them; they are not committed to the service of God, neither do they humble themselves before the almighty of God. They demand for only physical things instead of humbly asking for forgiveness of sins. The Son did not demand for food or anything else. He wanted forgiveness, a relationship with the father. He ended up getting more than he requested. He received the material capital (food, clothing etc.), Social capital (relationship) and the spiritual capital (forgiveness and cleansing of guilt). Seek first the kingdom of God and His righteousness and all other things shall be added to you (Matthew 6:33).

The cleansing of guilt: God cleansed the son before he could fellowship with him. In the same way, the blood of Jesus cleanses us if we sincerely confess our sins (1 John 1:5-10). God stands ready to forgive all who will turn to him. There is healing in forgiveness. Acts 3:19 says 'repent, then, and turn to God, so that your sins may be wiped out, that times of refreshing may come from the Lord'.

The celebration- God was happy when the lost son returned. There is rejoicing in heaven when one sinner repents (Luke 15:10). This is the heart of God. The book of 1 Timothy 2:3-4 says' this is good, and pleases God our Savior, who wants all men to be saved and to come to a knowledge of the truth'.

The rights of the saints: people who serve faithfully like the older son have the right to demand justice from God. It is very interesting to note that when the older brother became angry and refused to go into the house, the father went out to him and pleaded with him to come home. I call this 'the demands of the saints'. The Father knew that the older son was right in demanding justice. In Revelation 6:9-11, we can see a similar situation there:

> When he opened the fifth seal, I saw under the altar the souls of those who had been slain because of the word of God and the testimony they had maintained. They called out in a loud voice, How long, Sovereign Lord, holy and true, until you judge the inhabitants of the earth and avenge our blood? Then each of them was given a white robe, and they were told to wait a little longer, until the number of their fellow servants and brothers who were to be killed as they had been was completed.

The saints, who served God well in their lifetime, are demanding justice from God in heaven. They want God to punish the people who have been persecuting and killing Christians. And God will grant them their request at the right time. In the same way, you can also petition God to intervene on your behalf with those who have not treated you fairly. God is a just God! Romans 12: 17-19 says:

> Do not repay anyone evil for evil. Be careful to do what is right in the eyes of everybody. If it is possible, as far as it depends on you, live at peace with everyone. Do not take revenge, my friends, but leave room for God's wrath, for it is written: "It is mine to avenge; I will repay," says the Lord.

Do not worry if someone is treating you badly. As far as it depends on you, live at peace with everybody and continue to do good. At the right time God will deal with them for you! Someone once said this: 'No need for revenge - Just sit back and wait...those that hurt you will eventually screw up all by themselves and if you are lucky, God will let you watch'.

In this section, we have looked at how the abundance of material capital can also challenge some people to embark on a wrong journey of life; of moving far away from God, their creator. We used the life of the prodigal son as a case study. He made the wrong choice for leaving his father to a distant country for pleasure. The good news is that when he came to his senses he returned to his father, after suffering from both material and spiritual poverty. There are troubles all around; God will bring you out from your distress if, and only if you choose to draw closer to him. James 4:8 says 'Come near to God and he will come near to you. Wash your hands, you sinners, and purify your hearts, you double-minded'.

How can you know that you are closer to God or that you are far away from God? Fellowship! Fellowship! Fellowship! 1 John 1:3 says, 'We proclaim to you what we have seen and heard, so that you also may have fellowship with us. And our fellowship is with the Father and with his Son, Jesus Christ. Having fellowship with God, Jesus, and other believers in the church is one of the signs that you are closer with God. Therefore, make the worship of God in the church a priority. Make the worship of God in private a priority; and worship God in the public space as well. Is the path you are on leading you nearer to God, your creator, or farther away from God your creator?

3.3 Discovering the best direction in life

Getting the right information is very important in life. This section will discuss some of the guidelines that can help in discovering the best direction for life. Finding the right direction in life is an existential problem that all of us will face at some point time in life. Lack of direction, not lack of time, is the problem. We all have twenty-four hours in a day.' While some make good use of it, others have wasted every bit of it. There are many benefits in discovering the direction of your life and making it a priority. For me, discovering the right direction in life helped me to use my resources wisely, made me more focused, and gave me a sense purpose and a peaceful of mind.

There are many criteria people use to define the direction of their life. To some people, 'The first step in considering direction whether it's for your life as a whole, or your career, is to know what you want. Who do you want to become? Others too use soul searching technique for finding their direction in life. In this section, I will be discussing some of the criteria or guidelines for discovering the best direction in life.

Life guide one: The wide and narrow road of life

There are many sayings or quotes about the road of life. Most of these quotes can be helpful pointers, at least directing people the way forward, whether in a positive direction or in a negative direction. Most of these sayings about life are based on people's life experiences. For example, someone who is a financial guru will prefer this quote about the road of life: '*A good financial plan is a road map that shows us exactly how the choices we make today will affect our future*'. Many psychologists will find Sigmund Freud's saying inspiring: '*The interpretation of dreams is the royal road to knowledge of the unconscious activities of the mind.*' Sigmund Freud's is known as the father of psychoanalysis. Jesus Christ, the incarnate son of God, is 'the way, the truth and the life'

(John 14:6). Therefore His view about which direction to take is the best because He knows the 'in' and 'out' of this world. In *The Beatitudes* (a sermon encouraging beautiful attitudes) Jesus says:

> Jesus answered, I am the way and the truth and the life. No one comes to the Father except through me (John 14:6).

Thank God there is only one way to heaven, and this road is described by Jesus as very narrow. The other road is broad, but leads to destruction. What is this narrow way? Jesus Christ, describes himself as this way:

> Enter through the narrow gate. For wide is the gate and broad is the road that leads to destruction, and many enter through it. But small is the gate and narrow the road that leads to life, and only a few find it (Matthew 7:13-14).

Jesus Christ is this narrow way. John 8:12 tells us that 'When Jesus spoke again to the people, he said, "I am the light of the world. Whoever follows me will never walk in darkness, but will have the light of life'. When you follow this narrow way, you will never walk in darkness. Also, since Jesus is the bread of life (John 6:35), you are assured never to be hungry, both spiritually and physically. 'Jesus further declared, 'For my Father's will is that everyone who looks to the Son and believes in him shall have eternal life, and I will raise him up at the last day' (John 6:40).

The narrow way Jesus describes offers many benefits, but the most important one is that it leads to the life everlasting. By believing in Jesus Christ, and accepting him as Lord and saviour, repenting of your sins, and being baptized in the name of the Lord Jesus, and aiming to live a godly life, you are on the way leading to everlasting. It is the beginning of discovering who you are and why God created you in the way He did. Since the road is narrow, it is importance to be led, because there are many challenges on the road.

Life guide Two: Being led by the Spirit of God

God is very pleased to provide us with all the resources we need to live a victorious life here on earth and also ultimately make it to heaven (2

Peter 1:3). There are natural or earthly things; and there are spiritual or heavenly things (1 Corinthians 15:40). But you can rightfully access the divine provisions (heavenly things) God has made available to humanity if you allow yourself to be led by the Spirit of God. St. Paul tells those who have received God's Spirit that: 'We have not received the spirit of the world but the Spirit who is from God, that we may understand what God has freely given us. This is what we speak, not in words taught us by human wisdom but in words taught by the Spirit, expressing spiritual truths in spiritual words. The man without the Spirit does not accept the things that come from the Spirit of God, for they are foolishness to him, and he cannot understand them, because they are spiritually discerned' (1 Corinthians 2:12-14).

Those who will give their lives to God have one big assurance that, in this journey of life they are never alone. We have more than 365 scripture verses that assure us that God is with us. Jesus gave this assurance to the early church before He went to heaven. 'And I will ask the Father, and He will give you another Counselor to be with you forever; the Spirit of truth' (John 14:16-17). A counselor is an individual who guides people through their process of decision making. John 16:13 tells us that 'But when he, the Spirit of truth, comes, he will guide you into all the truth. He will not speak of his own; he will speak only what which he hears, and he will tell you what is yet to come'. There are many things we do not know in life yet. But those who will be led by Spirit of God will discover many helpful things in life. In the book of Isaiah, the scripture says, 'and your ears shall hear a word behind you, saying, "This is the way, walk in it," when you turn to the right or when you turn to the left' (Isaiah, 30:21). God does not send us on a journey and let us embark on it on our own.

Due to changing circumstances, the journey of life and serving God can be very demanding, and sometimes tiring. This is the main reason why we have the assurance in Acts 1:8, that we will receive power after the Holy Spirit has come upon us. For our weapon of warfare, the scripture says are not carnal but mighty through God, to the pulling down of stronghold (2

Corinthians, 2:4). To think we are able to succeed in this journey on our own strength is to concede defeat from before the start.

Anything you do in this life in the name of God, for God and others is a service to God. God thus has the responsibility to see you through. Witnessing Christ to other people is one of the important services to God. This is because, through witnessing, souls are won back to the Kingdom of God by receiving the salvation of their soul. According to Acts 1:8, when God's spirit comes on you, you become his ambassador, witnessing Christ from Jerusalem (your immediate place of abode, family and city) and Judea (your country), Samaria (your uncomfortable places) and to the ends of the world.

The Spirit of God also comes to empower us and give us boldness. When you are in need of self-discipline, or if you are timid, there is remedy in the 'Holy Spirit-package'. 2 Timothy 1: 7-8 tells us that 'For God did not give us a spirit of timidity, but a spirit of power, of love and of self-discipline. So do not be ashamed to testify about our Lord, or ashamed of me his prisoner. But join with me in suffering for the gospel, by the power of God, who has saved us and called us to a holy life—not because of anything we have done but because of his own purpose and grace. Those on the narrow road of life will receive a spirit of power, love and self-discipline to overcome any behavioral challenges they may have in order to become ambassadors of God.

Again, the Holy Spirit comes to bear fruit in us. The fruit of the Spirit scripture says is love, joy, peace, patience, kindness, goodness, faithfulness, gentleness and self-control. Against such things there is no law (Galatians 5: 22-24). These fruit are what distinguishes the believer from the unbeliever. Those who belong to Christ Jesus have crucified the sinful nature with its passions and desires' (Galatians, 5:24). Those who do not exhibit the fruit of the Spirit will manifest the deeds of the sinful nature. Galatians 5:19-21 says, 'the acts of the sinful nature are manifest: sexual immorality, impurity and debauchery; idolatry and witchcraft; hatred, discord, jealousy, fits of rage, selfish ambition, dissensions, factions and envy; drunkenness, orgies, and the like. I warn you, as I did before, that those who live like this will not inherit the kingdom of God'. Those who manifest these deeds, the scripture says are on the broad way that leads to eternal destruction.

In this section we have looked at the second guideline for discovering the best direction of life- to be led by the Spirit of God. Make a decision today to be led by the Spirit of God and your life will never be the same! Acts 2:36-47 can show you how to receive the Spirit of God so that you can also be led by the Spirit of God.

Life guide Three: Making the Kingdom of God a Priority

We have been looking at how to discover the best direction in life. We have so far discussed two guidelines; namely treading on the narrow way of life which is Jesus Christ, and being led by the spirit of God. The next guideline to be discussed under this heading is to encourage you to make the Kingdom of God a priority in your life. Live for God's kingdom, this is one of the best ways to live your life. Let us read Jesus' sayings on this theme:

> Then Jesus said to his disciples: "Therefore I tell you, do not worry about your life, what you will eat; or about your body, what you will wear. Life is more than food, and the body more than clothes. Consider the ravens: They do not sow or reap, they have no storeroom or barn; yet God feeds them. And how much more valuable you are than birds! Who of you by worrying can add a single hour to his life? Since you cannot do this very little thing, why do you worry about the rest? "Consider how the lilies grow. They do not labor or spin. Yet I tell you, not even Solomon in his entire splendor was dressed like one of these. If that is how God clothes the grass of the field, which is here today, and tomorrow is thrown into the fire, how much more will he clothe you, O you of little faith! And do not set your heart on what you will eat or drink; do not worry about it. For the pagan world runs after all such things, and your Father knows that you need them. But seek his kingdom, and these things will be given to you as well. Do not be afraid, little flock, for your Father has been pleased to give you the kingdom (Luke 12:22-32).

Seek ye first the kingdom of God and its righteousness and all other things shall be added to you. The kingdom of God seems to be one of the common themes in this book. Let us look at some of the importance of making God's kingdom a priority in life. We will consider the case of the believer first; when a believer first seeks the kingdom of God, he or she receives all other things according to the will and purposes of God; food, shelter, protection peace, children, career, eternal life etc (Matthew 6:33). God becomes your provider: 'and my God will meet all your needs according to the riches of his glory in Christ Jesus' says the apostle Paul in Philippians 4:19. Seeking God's kingdom first is a condition to receive help from above to overcome worry. Jesus says do not worry about anything, but seek God's kingdom first and the source of your worry will be taken care of by God. In practice, how can one seek the kingdom of God first?

Praying to God regularly, studying his word and practising what the scriptures say, attending church services, helping others, aiming to live a holy life, witnessing to others about the Lord Jesus Christ and inviting them to fellowship, making financial donations to support the kingdom work. These are steps in the right direction for Christians journeying on the way to God, and making the kingdom of God a life priority.

    For the unbeliever, the kingdom message is a message of hope, moving them from the kingdom of darkness to the kingdom of light (Colossians 1:13); from being an enemy of God to becoming his friend (Ephesians 2). This is the unbeliever's transformation from a state of hopelessness to hope, from hell to heaven, and from spiritual poverty to the glorious riches in Christ Jesus. It is a devastating thing to live the life without Christ. In the book of Matthew 9:35-38, Jesus compares people without God to Sheep without a shepherd:

> Jesus went through all the towns and villages, teaching in their synagogues, preaching the good news of the kingdom and healing every disease and sickness. When he saw the crowds, he had compassion on them, because they were harassed and helpless, like sheep without a shepherd. Then he said to his disciples, "The harvest is plentiful but the workers are few. Ask the Lord of the harvest, therefore, to send out workers into his harvest field.

In this account, Jesus was touched with a feeling of miserable condition of the people; he resolved to provide some remedy for them, directing his disciples to intercede that God should send forth labourers into his harvest field. We will discuss the importance of training more ministers of the gospel and missions shortly. But let us first reflect on the verse 38: 'When he saw the crowds, he had compassion on them, because they were harassed and helpless, like sheep without a shepherd' (Luke 10:38).

People without God can be compared to sheep without a shepherd. In the eyes of God, they are aimless and lost about their purpose in life. For a created human being to deny or denounce his creator can be compared to a little Chick that decides to live apart from the mother hen in spite of the looming presence of the Hawk. Such people are always exposed to continual danger without protection; they can be harassed by wicked principalities and demons including Satan himself (1 Peter 5:8). What makes their condition even worse is the fact that, in spite of this, eternal condemnation awaits such people. Many people, out of frustration have turned to wrong places for help, but they have not been successful. The apostle Paul lamented in his frustration, but he found help when he looked up to Jesus Christ. He says this in Romans 7:24-25 'What a wretched man I am! Who will rescue me from this body of death? Thanks be to God—through Jesus Christ our Lord'.

Concerning the need to train more labourers for the Kingdom work, we will recall Jesus' saying that the gospel of the kingdom of God must be preached in the whole world before the end will come (Matthew 24:14). This is one of the reasons why the church is required to train more pastors and missionaries to take the kingdom message to all people for their deliverance and salvation. What role are you playing towards the sharing of the gospel message? You can help by telling people close to you about the good news of God's kingdom and invite them to church. You can also encourage friends and family members to become pastors and missionaries or you can make financial donation to help train more church workers and to help send missionaries to share the gospel and to plant churches. Let us win souls and fill our churches with men and women who are born again.

What do people know about the Kingdom of God? Daniel 2:44 tells us that:

> In the time of those kings, the God of heaven will set up a kingdom that will never be destroyed, nor will it be left to another people. It will crush all those kingdoms and bring them to an end, but it will itself endure forever.

Accordingly, God's kingdom was set up during the days of the last of these kingdoms, that is, during the Roman Empire. What is God's kingdom? It is the reign of God in the life of people now and in the new world to come (Luke 17:20-21). We will discuss this subject further in this section.

Why did God establish His kingdom? The purpose of the coming of God's kingdom according to scripture is first to defeat (crush) the enemies of God. Daniel 2:44 tells us that God's kingdom 'will crush all other kingdoms and bring them to an end, but it will itself endure forever'. Any human kingdom which existed before and after the coming of God's kingdom will be defeated. On another level, there are some little kingdoms in people's lives such as sin, infirmities, addictions, evil spirits, death etc. which God's kingdom came to defeat. Anything that has a hold of your life in a negative way can be considered as reigning in your life. According to 1 Corinthians 15:26 the last enemy to be destroyed is death. The resurrection of Jesus from the dead is a demonstration of one of the agendas of the kingdom of God. The book Acts 2:24 tells us that 'But God raised him [Jesus] from the dead, freeing him from the agony of death, because it was impossible for death to keep its hold on him. Do you know that the last enemy to be destroyed is death? Read 1 Corinthians 15:26.

In the course of his life on earth, Jesus exercised a prerogative as a son of God by raising Lazarus from the death and made this declaration afterwards: 'I am the resurrection and the life. He who believes in me will live, even though he dies; and whoever lives and believes in me will never die (John 11:25-26). Do you believe this?

Jesus equally said in Mathew 12:28: 'But if it is by the Spirit of God that I drive out demons, then the kingdom of God has come upon you'.

With this, we can define the Kingdom of God as the reign of God in people's life on this earth and in the new world to come' (Luke 11:20). Having been asked by the Pharisees when the kingdom of God would come, Jesus replied, The kingdom of God does not come with your careful observation, nor will people say, here it is, or there it is, the kingdom of God is within you' (Luke 17:20-21). It is my pray that God's kingdom will defeat any negative thing in your life including sickness, evil spirits, bad people, emotional stress , sin etc.

The second reason for the coming of the kingdom of God is that, it comes to restore what has been lost. God's intention for us is good, but 'the devil came to steal, to kill and to destroy', Jesus came so that we will have abundant life' (John, 10:10). The devil has stolen good things from many people, and so those who are privileged to have the reign of God in their lives receive back whatever Satan has stolen in their lives. For example, Luke 13:10-17 tells the healing story of a woman 'whom Satan had kept bound for eighteen long years'. Like this woman, receive your healing as you read this book in Jesus name.

The third reason for the coming of the kingdom of God is that, it comes to show us a better way to live our lives. Jesus tells us in Luke 22:24-30 that service and humility are the means to become great in the kingdom of God. In Luke 12:15, Jesus also tells us how to be content in life: 'Watch out! Be on your guard against all kinds of greed; a man's life does not consist in the abundance of his possessions." The apostle Paul echoed this; 'for we brought nothing into the world, and we can take nothing out of it. But if we have food and clothing, we will be content with that. People who want to get rich fall into temptation and a trap into many foolish and harmful desires that plunge men into ruin and destruction. Mark 1:14-15, tells us that 'After John was put in prison, Jesus went into Galilee, proclaiming the good news of God. The time has come, he said. The kingdom of God is near. Repent and believe the good news! It is this Kingdom we are all called to make it a priority in our lives because of the many benefits it has for humanity.

In this chapter, we have discussed three main guidelines for discovering the best direction in life. The narrow way which is Jesus Christ;

the Holy Spirit leading the way; and making the kingdom of God a priority. The next chapter discusses how we can prioritize sacred things and common things in life.

Chapter 4

Prioritising sacred things & common things

In this chapter, we will look at three categories of sacred things in our world and suggest ways of approaching them so that you can be blessed by them. These are: God, certain people and certain items. Sacredness is defined as something or someone worthy of worship; very holy, set apart for service to God, or highly valued and important, deserving respect. The Sacred things or people or deity are selectively chosen to be a blessing to 'common' things or people. Without the existence of common things, there would not be the need for sacred things on earth. Some people have been divinely set apart for specific task in this world. Their purpose in this world is to accomplish specific task for the betterment of humanity to the glory of God. When you come across any sacred people or object, begin to think of giving that person or object a high priority. This is because they have the potential to influence your future endeavours.

Sadly, many people disrespect or treat things which are meant to be a blessing to them with contempt to their own detriment. It is difficult to receive blessings or benefits from that which we do not have regard or respect for. For example, marriage and family life are sacred and are meant to be a blessing. But when couples decide, or treat marriage with levity, they do not gain the blessing that comes with it. Many couples unfortunately, do not respect their vows and the sacredness of their marriage and so they end up destroying rather than benefiting from their marriages.

The monster that consumes itself is a classic example. In their book, *Spiritual Capital; the wealth we can live by,* Danah Zohar and Ian Marshall tell a story from Greek mythology about a wealthy timber merchant called Erisychthon (pronounce as Er-ris-ya-thon). Erisychthon is a greedy man who only thinks of profit. Nothing is sacred to him. On Erisychthon's land, there is a special tree beloved of the gods. Prayers of the saints are tied to its prodigious branches and spirits dance round its magnificent trunk. Erisychthon cares nothing about this fact. He looks at the tree, and assesses the volume of timber it will produce, and then he takes an axe to it. Against all caution and protest, he chops until the tree is withered and fallen, and all divine life that inhabited the tree has left. But one of the gods puts a curse on Erisychthon for his greed. From that day forward, Erisychthon is consumed by an insatiable hunger. He begins by eating all his stores then he turns all his wealth into food he can consume. Still not satisfied, he consumes his wife and children. In the end, Erisychthon is left with nothing to consume but his own flesh. He eats himself! Erisychthon is a symbol that may represent the self-destructive fate not just of business but of our whole culture if we allow the narrow values of today's short-term, money-obsessed world to dominate our broader lives and choices. Self-centred people are likely to disrespect sacred things.

4.1 God is sacred

God, the creator of the universe is sacred. This means a lot to us all. The sacredness of God means He is set apart, holy, worthy of worship. As I said earlier on, sacred beings or things are meant to be a blessing to us. If you give God the due reverence, this will attract divine blessings from heaven into your life. To have disregard for the creator God is tantamount to incurring his displeasure. But to acknowledge and heed his commands is to put one in a positive stead for his untold blessings.

But how can one respect, and keep God's commandment? Exodus 20:7 says 'You shall not misuse the name of the LORD your God, for the LORD will not hold anyone guiltless who misuses his name'. One of the ways we disregard God is through ingratitude. Let us honor God in all our ways. Another way we disrespect God is through harming or insulting our fellow human beings. This is evident in the following scriptures; Proverbs 14:31, 'he who oppresses the poor shows contempt for their Maker, but whoever is kind to the needy honors God'. He who mocks the poor shows contempt for their Maker' (Proverbs 17:5).

1 Timothy 6:16 says God alone is immortal and lives in unapproachable light. Because God is Holy, many people prefer to live a life without him. But getting closer to God through prayers, fellowship, reading of the scriptures will nourish our soul. Ravi Zacharias has observed the following:

> Pleasure without God, without the sacred boundaries, will actually leave you emptier than before. This is biblical truth; this is also an experiential truth. The loneliest people in the world are amongst the wealthiest and the most famous who found no boundaries within which to live. That is a fact I've

We should acknowledge God in everything, and then we will be fulfilled. As Ravi has rightly observed, living without God will make you emptier, even in times of pleasure. Many people are not happy despite their achievements and the material things they have acquired. These people should turn to God. Similar testimonies come from internationally known psychiatrists. Carl Jung a distinguish psychiatrists once said, 'The central neurosis of our time is emptiness'. A supporting diagnosis came from Vicktor Frankl, who said that 'clinics are crowded with people suffering from a new kind or neurosis, a sense of total and ultimate meaningless of life'. This frustration has come because men and women have an inherent tendency to reach out for meanings to fulfil and values to actualize. 'No physician however has diagnosed the sickness of the soul without faith'. Living without God can also make us vulnerable, and exposes us to forces of evil in the world. Read what Cain said when he was driven from the presence of God because of his murderous act against his brother Abel. Cain said to the LORD, 'my punishment is more than I can bear. Today you are driving me from the land, and I will be hidden from your presence; I will be a restless wanderer on the earth, and whoever finds me will kill me' (Genesis 4:13-14). A life without God can be frustrating. As Danah Zohar noted in her book, it is essential to be aware of the recent discovery of the 'God spot', a mass of neural tissues on the brain's temporal lobes that enables human beings to have a sense of the sacred and a longings for the deeper things in life. So please don't suppress this desire for God. The God spot accounts for the presence of religious ideas, rites, and rituals since the founding of the earliest known human societies. To live without God is to deny yourself the best of life.

4.2 Certain People are Sacred

What I mean by the statement 'certain people are sacred' is that some people have been divinely set apart for specific task in this world. Their purpose in this word is to accomplish specific task for the betterment of humanity to the glory of God. Examples include the prophets of God, parents, people in authority, and spiritual heads. They have specifically significant role to play in individual and community life, and anyone could fit into this criteria if they will cleanse themselves from unworthy lifestyle, they can become an instrument for noble purposes, made holy, useful to the Master and prepared to do any good work (2 Tim 2:21) . Rise up and be a blessing to your generation.

But the fact that these people have been set apart for specific purposes does not immune them from life realities or God's judgment. They are all required, like everyone else to give an account to God for their stewardship (Romans 2:6-11). I must also state here again that the fact that someone is chosen for a specific task by God does not necessarily mean they will automatically go to heaven no matter the outcome of their life. To go to heaven is a decision everyone must make for themselves. God does the chosen for a particular service or task on earth, we decide whether we want to be with him in heaven or not.

God can use 'anything' as instrument in his missions, so be careful and humble yourself. In 1 king 17:2-6, God instructed a bird to go and feed the prophet Elijah. In Luke, 19:40 Jesus says, He can even cause stones to do his praises. In Joshua chapter 2, a harlot named Rahab welcomed God's servants and provided a secure place for them on their mission. References to Rahab elsewhere in the Bible show that she gained a unique place in the history of Christianity. She and her family alone survived the destruction of

Jericho. By marrying a man named Salmon (possibly a relative of the hero Caleb), she became a direct ancestress of Jesus Christ (Matthew 1:5). The authors of James (James 2:25) and Hebrews (Hebrews 11:31) hold up Rahab as an example of faith.

In the book of Daniel 2:36-38, God gave dominion and power, might and glory to the heathen king, Nebuchadnezzar. In his hands God placed mankind and the beasts of the field and the birds of the air. Wherever they live, God made him ruler over them all. The point here is that God can use anything of his creation to be a blessing to the world. In such situations, the vessels then become sacred, deserving special respect. I believe if God can use anything for His mission on earth, then He can certainly use you as well for greater works no matter your background. I believe this calls for a humble spirit as well. For, you never know what vessel God will use to bless you. If God used a bird to feed the prophet Elijah in a famine season, then He can use anything to bless you as well.

The calling forth of the nation Israel is an example in point. The nation of Israel was chosen by God to be a light to the world (Isaiah 49:6). They were the recipients of the divine knowledge about God to be shared with the rest of humankind. They were also chosen to preserve a race or a group of people through whom the Messiah (Jesus Christ) came to bring salvation to the rest of the world (Romans 9:3-5). Salvation of the human soul through faith in Jesus is from the Jews to the gentiles. That is why the apostle Paul could say that 'I am not ashamed of the gospel, because it is the power of God for the salvation of everyone who believes: first for the Jew, then for the Gentile' (Romans 1:16).

Someone may ask what standard(s) does God uses to select these 'sacred people'. Others may equally ask, whether these people are chosen before they were born or whether they are chosen as a result of their good deeds? Jeremiah 1:4-5 tells us this:

> The word of the LORD came to me, saying, before I formed you in the womb I knew you, before you were born I set you apart; I appointed you as a prophet to the nations.

From this text, we are made to understand that God's purposes concerning us have been predestined before our very existence. Ephesians 2:10 also tells us that ' For we are God's workmanship, created in Christ Jesus to do good works, which God prepared in advance for us to do'. So, if you are living a bad lifestyle now, know that your true lifestyle is to be a work person of God created in Christ Jesus to do good works. This is your original purpose as ordained by God, your creator. But the question is, can this be said of everybody? Did God have a specific job description for everybody before God formed them in the womb? Yes, God has a purpose for every individual in the world, and by extension, everything He created. So the sea, the birds that fly, the living and the non-living are God's ultimate plans for his creation. 2 Timothy 2:20-21 tells us this:

> In a large house there are articles not only of gold and silver, but also of wood and clay; some are for noble purposes and some for ignoble. If a man cleanses himself from the latter, he will be an instrument for noble purposes, made holy, useful to the Master and prepared to do any good work.

God has already set everyone apart for a specific task. Our own task is to draw near to him so we could discover this purpose and walk in it. I must also admit that, sometimes it is difficult to understand how God does certain things. God says His ways are not our ways and His thoughts not our thought (Isaiah 55:8-9). So we have to draw closer to Him, and clean ourselves from sin to be able to fit into the use for his noble purposes. I pray God shows His ways to you as you read this book.

    Jesus Christ, the only begotten Son of God, was sent into this world to save sinners. For no one is qualified to be the saviour of this world, except Jesus Christ (John 14:6). John 3:16 is the Gospel in a Nutshell. 'For God so loved the world that he gave his one and only Son, that whoever believes in him shall not perish but have eternal life. This Bible verse has probably been memorized more than any other verse in the Bible. In a few words, it tells the story of salvation: God's love for the world, God's gift of his Son, and the opportunity for anyone who believes to be saved. Give Jesus Christ the due reverence today. He invites all who are burdened to come to Him to rest (Matthew 11:28-29).

Even those of you who are not familiar with the Bible can note this fact in the society that certain people are specifically selected and trained to do certain specific tasks or assignments that no one else can do except them. But the church has a special role in this world as well. In addition for being the light and the salt of the world (Matthew 5:13-16), the church also has an ambassadorial role in preaching a message of reconciliation between God and sinners (2 Corinthians 5:18-21). In the present time, it is the church and the Spirit of God that give invitation to people in the world to come to God, the fountain of life. You have a duty to worship the God who created you. It is the duty of the church to tell you about this God until you know this God for yourself. Revelation 22:17 says:

> The Spirit and the bride [the church] say, Come! And let him who hears say, Come! Whoever is thirsty, let him come; and whoever wishes, let him take the free gift of the water of life (Revelation 22:17).

Ephesians 3:10-12 also tells us that God's intention was that now, through the church, the manifold wisdom of God should be made known to the rulers and authorities in the heavenly realms, according to his eternal purpose which he accomplished in Christ Jesus our Lord. In him and through faith in him we may approach God with freedom and confidence. Because the church has such a special role towards God and for the world, the church is a sacred body, which demands deep respect. But what do we see these days? What do people say about the church? Many people do not respect the church. The church has many roles to play in the world. The church is there, to lead people to God and to help them nourish their faith, providing a place where sinners could come to.

We can attract blessings from these people by honouring them with our substances, and by being obedient to the word of God they tell us, and not speaking ill of them. God said to Abraham, I will bless those who will bless you, and curse those who will curse you (Genesis 12:3). When you come across someone chosen by God to do a specific task, please bless that person else, leave that person alone. God says 'Do not touch my anointed ones; do my prophets no harm' (psalm 105:15). Genesis 20 tells us of a king who attempted to take Abraham's wife Sarah. The Bible says, God appeared to this king in his dream and warned him to return the woman to Abraham. Remember that Abraham walked faithfully with God, and God called him His friend (James 2:23). Never think of harming anybody in this world especially, a sacred person. The book of 2 Kings 2 gives an account of a prophet of God who called wild animals to maul a large gang of teenagers who were mocking the prophet of God:

> From there Elisha went up to Bethel. As he was walking along the road, some youths came out of the town and jeered at him. "Go on up, you baldhead!" they said. Go on up, you baldhead! He turned around, looked at them and called down a curse on them in the name of the LORD. Then two bears came out of the woods and mauled forty-two of the youths (2 Kings 2:23-24).

Reading this account at first glance could be very worrying; a prophet calling on bears to maul children? However, putting the text in its historical context paints a different picture. Bethel later on became a hotbed of Baal worship, and its residents were engaged in a life-and-death struggle with the true prophets of God. When the youths called out, 'Go on up, you baldhead!' that was an insult, they were calling for Elisha to vanish into the sky, or in other words, to die. In actuality, a large gang of teenagers was threatening a prophet's life. Elisha cursed them, calling forth a bear to attack. Elisha was a prophet to the nation Israel. If you have nothing good to say about God's people, please leave them alone and attend to your own business.

Nothing stirs a nation's blood like a liberator. The United States remembers two especially: Washington and Lincoln. George Washington led the original fight for independence. A century later, Abraham Lincoln set three million slave people free. For those slaves, Lincoln was a true liberator. In India, a scrawny little man named Gandhi Mahatma is acknowledged for leading his people to freedom. For the Israelites, Moses' name continues to ring a bell, and many biblical passages have been devoted to narrating the story of this great prophet of God. Ultimately, Jesus came as the great Liberator who came to set all humanity free.

Going back to Moses, in the context of the Jewish nation, the New Testament reached back to him for a comparison (Hebrews 3:1-6). History is a particular account we can learn from. Moses was born at a time when the King of Egypt had ordered that every male child below the age of two be killed (Exodus 2). But because Moses was destined for a specific task, no amount of effort by the king of Egypt could destroy the baby Moses. Moses grew up and led Israel out of Egypt. In the same way, if God has destined you for a specific task, be rest assured, nothing will be able to destroy you as long as you continue to trust in God.

Historical precedence and experience have shown how unwise it is for anyone to work or unnecessarily oppose 'sacred people'. They have special grace to bless. Because of their unique assignment on earth, God himself deals with whoever tries to make these sacred people's work difficult. My advice to anyone reading this book is that you should never work to frustrate people who are doing something good for humanity, but that you should rather support them. Some of the very people God sent Moses to liberate did not relate appropriately with Moses. The result was that, God punished them, some of them received leprosy, and some too were destroyed.

We will consider Miriam, Moses elder sister as a case in point in Numbers 12. She did not give Moses the respect due him. Among life's most difficult tasks is enjoying the success of a brother or sister who outdoes you. Certainly Moses' sister Miriam found it difficult. At Moses' birth she was the hero, watching over her baby brother and cleverly jumping in to outwit Pharaoh's daughter. Miriam, Moses' older sister, had helped saved his life when he was a baby (Exodus 2:7). She took the spotlight again when the Israelites crossed the Red Sea, leading the women in a wild song of triumph (Exodus 15:20). As a prophetess, Miriam played an important leadership role alongside Moses, who carried the chief responsibilities. Then jealousy crept in. Miriam and her brother Aaron, another strong leader, began to grumble against Moses unnecessarily.

They objected to Moses' wife, a foreigner, and they felt they ought to have equal spiritual status with Moses. 'Has the LORD indeed spoken only through Moses? They asked. Has He not spoken through us as well?' (Numbers. 12:2). Miriam and her brother Aaron felt some sibling rivalry for their kid brother. Irked by his foreign wife, they began undercutting his leadership by asking whether he had a monopoly on God's will. Moses apparently did not defend himself, but God came to his defense with scathing words that made clear their special relationship. God responded with a fierce anger: "How dare you? 'Why then were you not afraid to speak against my servant Moses? The anger of the LORD burned against them, and he left them. When the cloud lifted from above the Tent, there stood Miriam—leprous, like snow. Aaron turned toward her and saw that she had leprosy; and he said to Moses, 'Please, my lord, do not hold against us the sin we have so foolishly committed'. God singled out Miriam, apparently the leader of the two, for punishment.

What many people do not know is that leaders are always under tremendous pressure from their duties and the task ahead of them. They do not really enjoy the material blessings they seem to have. They may appear popular, seem to have opportunities in life than others, but all these seem nothing to them. They are always under pressure carrying the burdens of the people. Unfortunately, many church leaders behave like Miriam and Aaron. They oppose, unnecessarily and fight their leaders. Life Questions: What makes you jealous? How can you best handle those jealous feelings towards those whom God has chosen for specific task? We can learn how to wisely relate to 'sacred people' by looking at the encounter between Abraham and Melchizedek recorded in Genesis 14:18-20:

> Then Melchizedek king of Salem brought out bread and wine. He was priest of God Most High, and he blessed Abram, saying, "Blessed be Abram by God Most High, Creator of heaven and earth. And blessed be God Most High, who delivered your enemies into your hand. Then Abram gave him a tenth of everything.

When you meet someone of a higher spiritual authority what do you do? In this encounter, Abraham had returned from war, and met this enigmatic priest. This priest blessed Abraham spiritually while Abraham blessed him with material things; 'a tenth of the plunder'. There must be respect for 'sacred people' and vice versa. Both Abraham and Melchizedek were important and great men in their own calling, and both recognized that. In the same way, you may not be a priest, but in the eyes of the Lord you are important and have a specific assignment to accomplish in this world. Your duty is to draw closer to God in order to discover your purpose in this world.

Abraham was important first of all, simply because God chose him. Shortly after the destruction caused by the great flood, God picked Abraham as the foundation of a new humanity (Genesis 12). *The Mystery Man:* Melchizedek appeared to Abraham without warning, but received tremendous honor, and then disappeared. Yet centuries later, he was mention in Psalm 110, and subsequently in Hebrews 7:11-17. Melchizedek remains a mysterious figure, but he does set an important precedent for the Messiah- (the same man can serve as both priest and king). Please note that Jewish priests came from one tribe, and kings from another, different tribe. Though Melchizedek did not have the proper family lineage, his spiritual power impressed Abraham.

The angel Gabriel appeared to Mary to announce to her, her role as the mother of Jesus Christ. Mary respected the angel and welcomed the good news. Both Mary and the angel had unique assignments (Luke 1:26-38). There is an equally story between David the second King of Israel and Ahitophel which is deserving of a special attention in this section as well. Ahitophel of the house of Israel and Balaam of the heathen nations were the two great sages of the world, who failing to show gratitude to God for their wisdom, perished in dishonour. Ahitophel was a counsellor of King David and a man greatly renowned for his sagacity. At the time of Absalom's revolt[4], he deserted David and espoused the cause of Absalom (2 Samuel 15:12). David sent his old friend Hushai back to Absalom, in order that he

---

[4] Absalom, according to the Bible was the third son of David, King of Israel with Maachah, daughter of Talmai, 2 Samuel 14:25 describes him as the most handsome man in the kingdom. Unsuccessfully, Absalom staged a coup to remove his father David from the throne.

might counteract the counsel of Ahitophel (2 Samuel 15:31-37). Ahitophel, seeing that his good advice against David had not been followed due to Hushai's influence, left the camp of Absalom at once, returned to Giloh, his native place, and after arranging his worldly affairs, hanged himself, and was buried in the sepulcher of his fathers (2 Samuel 17:1-23). Ahitophel died a foolish death because he did not respect the kind who appointed him to leadership role.

In Rabbinical literature, the Talmud[5] speaks of Ahitophel as a man, like Balaam, whose great wisdom was not received in humility as a gift from heaven, and so, his wisdom became a stumbling-block to him (Num. R. xxii.). He was one of those who, while casting longing eyes upon things not belonging to them, equally lose the things they possess. Accordingly, Ahithophel was granted access by Almighty God into the Divine powers of the Holy Name (YHWH). And being thus familiar with divine wisdom and knowledge, he was consulted as an oracle like the Urim and Thummim (Numbers 27:21). But he withheld his mystic knowledge from King David in the hour of peril, and was therefore doomed to die from strangulation. The Bible says 'Anyone, then, who knows the good he ought to do and doesn't do it, sins' (James 4:14).

It is also said that David, during his reign, had many disagreeable encounters with Ahithophel. Shortly after his accession, King David seems to have overlooked Ahithophel in his appointments of judges and other officials. Consequently, when David was in despair concerning the visitation upon Uzzah during the attempted transport of the ark (2 Samuel 6:7) and sought counsel from Ahithophel, the latter mockingly suggested to him that he had better apply to his own wise men. Only upon David's malediction, that whoever knew a remedy and concealed it should surely end his life by committing suicide, did Ahithophel offer him some rather vague advice, concealing the true solution, which was that the ark must be carried on the shoulders of men instead of upon a wagon (1 Chronicles 15:15).

On another occasion, Ahithophel would only render a service to David after he had been threatened with a curse. It appears that David

---

[5]The *Talmud* is a vast collection of Jewish laws and traditions

excavated too deeply for the foundations of the Temple, with the result that the earth's deepest floods broke forth. None could help but Ahithophel, who withheld his counsel in the hope of seeing David borne away upon the flood. When David again warned him of the malediction, Ahithophel counselled the king to throw a tile, with the ineffable name of God (YHWH) written upon it, into the cavity; whereupon the waters began to sink. David's repeated malediction that Ahithophel would be hanged was finally realized when the latter hanged himself.

This is the drift of my discourse and the thrust of the analyses so far in this section. Anyone who intentionally works against a 'sacred person' may end up like Ahitophel. The Christian faith interpreters often see Ahithophel as an antitype of Judas Iscariot. Ahithophel's betrayal of David, and his subsequent suicide are seen as anticipating Judas' betrayal of Jesus, and the gospel's account of Judas hanging himself (Matthew 27:5). The book of Psalm 41:9, which seems to refer to Ahithophel, is quoted in John 13:18 as being fulfilled in Judas. Please if God grants you the opportunity to work or support a 'chosen person' on any mission, do not repeat the mistakes of Ahithophel and Judas. Some people know what they can do for their local church to grow but they will not do it. This is considered a sin before God: 'Anyone, then, who knows the good he ought to do and doesn't do it, sins' (James 4:17).

As already mentioned, the fact that these 'sacred people' have been set apart for specific purposes does not mean they are immune to life realities or judgment. They are all required, like everyone else to give an account to God for the things done in this world (Romans 2:6-11). When David sinned against God by taken someone's wife, he was severely disciplined by God (2 Samuel 12). The Lord used the Assyrians to discipline the nation Israel because of idolatry. But the Assyrians became wanted themselves because of pride, and so were punished by God (Isaiah 10:5-13). Centuries later the Lord, chose Nebuchadnezzar king of Babylon, and gave him authority over every nation of the world (Jeremiah 27:6-8).

Just like the king of Assyria, God disciplined Nebuchadnezzar when he became proud (Daniel, 4). Remember, God turned Nebuchadnezzar into a wild animal that lived in the forest for seven years, before turning him back again into human. He later praised God. This is how all those who will refuse to give honour to God will be treated one day. Romans 1:21 says 'For although they knew God, they neither glorified him as God nor gave thanks to him, but their thinking became futile and their foolish hearts were darkened.

A lot has been said about the fact that some people have been set apart for specific task for the betterment of humanity. Our aim should be to find out how best we can relate to these people as they come our way. Due to the fact that these people are 'sacred', my suggestion in this book is that we give them the maximum respect so that they can be a blessing to us. The special grace they carry is not for their private use, but for the common good of humanity. They are stewards, people God has entrusted treasures to, they will give an account to God one day. The fact that someone is chosen for a specific task by God does not necessarily mean they are safe and automatically safe in the judgment of God. God does the chosen for a particular service or task on earth, we decide whether we want to be with him in heaven or not.

4.3 Certain Objects & Places are Sacred

There are certain places that are Holy or sacred, set apart for special purpose, usually for divine purposes. And within the premises of these places, are items which are also set apart for specific use. Our aim in this section is to learn what to do when we come to such places or when we come into contact with these sacred items.

1. Certain Places are Sacred

The story of the prophet Moses and the burning bush tells us how one can easily come to or discover a sacred place in their day to day activities. In this incident Moses was tending the flock of Jethro his father-in-law, the priest of Midian, and he led the flock to the far side of the desert and came to Horeb:

> Moses saw that though the bush was on fire it did not burn up. So Moses thought, I will go over and see this strange sight—why the bush does not burn up. When the LORD saw that he had gone over to look, God called to him from within the bush, Moses! Moses! And Moses said, here I am. Do not come any closer, God said. Take off your sandals, for the place where you are standing is holy ground (Exodus 3:2-5).

God spoke to Moses from an unexpected source: a burning bush. When Moses saw it, he went to investigate. He was ordered to take off his shoes as an act of reverence before God. In fact some people still approach any Holy place such as church, mosque or shrine without any sandals. The question most people will ask is should we then remove our shoes anytime we have an encounter with God?

The practice of putting off one's shoe in certain places as a form of reverence was a culturally accepted practice in those days. This might not necessarily apply in our context since in our context, taking off one's shoe do not necessarily mean the same. But you can take off your shoes out of reverence for God. Holy ground, literally means "ground of holiness" - ground rendered holy by the presence of God upon it. The custom of treading barefoot in holy places seems to have been general in the East: the Egyptians used it: and Pythagoras, who recommends to his disciples to worship, putting off their shoes, is thought to have learned this rite from them. Some suggest that the rationale of it being that the shoes or sandals have dust or dirt attached to them, and thus, required to be taken off for the purpose of maintaining cleanliness. Henry observes that what represents putting off shoes then could be likened to one putting off the hat- a token of respect and submission[6].

Those who approach God without sandals does so for God and those who approach God with sandals equally does so for God provided they acknowledge his presence and have deep respect in their heart for God. We ought to approach God with a solemn pause and preparation; and to express our inward reverence by a grave and reverent behaviour in the worship of God, carefully avoiding everything that looks light or rude. God

---

[6] From Benson's Commentary

is our Father, but he is also our sovereign Lord. To approach him frivolously shows a lack of respect and sincerity. When you come to God in worship, do you approach him casually, or do you come as though you were an invited guest before the great King? If necessary adjust your attitude so that it is suitable for approaching a holy God. It was the presence of God that made the place a Holy or sacred place. From this incident, we can say that wherever God choose to come that place becomes a sacred place, where people present will be blessed. Another example can be found in Exodus 19:10-12:

> And the LORD said to Moses, Go to the people and consecrate them today and tomorrow. Have them wash their clothes and be ready by the third day, because on that day the LORD will come down on Mount Sinai in the sight of all the people. Put limits for the people around the mountain and tell them, 'Be careful that you do not go up the mountain or touch the foot of it. Whoever touches the mountain shall surely be put to death.

In this instance, the mountain became sacred only at the time God came on top of that mountain to speak to the people. There were even regulations as how the people were to approach the mountain because of the presence of God. As a matter of fact, the people were even asked to wash themselves and clean their clothes.

Always remember that, what makes a place sacred is the presence of God and where the presence of God is, uncommon miracles can take place. Luke 5:17 tells us that 'One day as He [Jesus] was teaching, the Pharisees and teachers of the law, who had come from every village of Galilee and from Judea and Jerusalem, were sitting there. And the power of the Lord was present for Him to heal the sick'. Here, what makes the healing of the sick possible was the presence of the Lord. The book of 2 Corinthians 3:17 also tells us that 'Now the Lord is the Spirit, and where the Spirit of the Lord is, there is freedom'. The presence of the Lord sets people free from any bondage they find themselves. It breaks every yoke, and every evil power that has gripped them. Learn to create an environment for the presence of God.

The meeting place of Christian believers is considered sacred because God has promised to come to his people wherever two or more of them have gather in his name (Matthew 18:20). There are also at times when God specifically chose a place for his presence to dwell there continuously or when someone or a group of people set a particular place apart specifically as a worship place; that place becomes a holy place for God.

Solomon's prayer in the book of 2 Chronicles 6 and God's response in the chapter 7 marked a high point in Israel's existence as a nation. United, the Israelites gathered before the gleaming new temple. God responded to Solomon's dedication prayers as follows:

> Now my eyes will be open and my ears attentive to the prayers offered in this place. I have chosen and consecrated this temple so that my Name may be there forever. My eyes and my heart will always be there (2 Chronicles 7:15-16).

This is the reason why believers dedicate their church buildings as places of worship to God. Those who take care of God's temple or the church building receive special blessings from heaven. On the other hand, worshippers who neglect the temple of God can sometimes be disciplined by God for treating his sacred place with contempt. Jesus took a drastic step when he saw that people were treating the temple of God with contempt:

> Jesus entered the temple area and drove out all who were buying and selling there. He overturned the tables of the money changers and the benches of those selling doves. It is written, he said to them, 'My house will be called a house of prayer,' but you are making it a 'den of robbers. The blind and the lame came to him at the temple, and he healed them (Matthew 21:12-14).

The moment the temple was cleansed sick people were healed at the same place. There is one important way in which Matthew's account differs from the rest of the gospels on Jesus' cleansing of the temple. The book of Mathew says that after the temple was cleansed, the blind and the lame came to Him at the temple, and He healed them (Matthew 21:14). This could suggest that God's presence and power to heal might suffer a bit of setback with the continuous presence of sin and a disregard for God. In Jesus' day, activities at the temple, supposedly the center for worship of God, had taken on a commercial cast. Merchants sold sacrificial animals to pilgrims and foreigners at inflated prices. The system was designed more for profit than for true worship. Jesus responded first by aggressively turning out these robbers, and then by turning his attention to the people with real needs, the blind and the lame.

There are robbers in today's church. There are people in the church who are messing up with the things of God. They thus prevent people with real needs to come to God to receive help from the great God, the Father of the universe. Unless the church is cleansed of hypocrisy, moral filth, idolatry, greed, sluggishness, etc. there could not be the move of God. Reforming the church has always been costly and uncomfortable, but at the end, it is the will of God that prevails.

Like Jesus, true children of God should work hard to keep the church cleansed for God's presence to dwell. One way we can make this happen is by keeping the sanctity of the house of God. Jesus himself did not allow people to turn the house of prayer into anything else. See His further warnings in the book of Revelation chapters 2 and 3. We should continue to listen to His warnings in our churches. Through prayer, worship, and the ministration of the sacraments and the word of God, we have fellowship with Him. 'Here I am! I stand at the door and knock. If anyone hears my voice and opens the door, I will come in and eat with him, and he with me' (Revelation 3:20).

In the New Testament, the emphasis on God's temple is both on the physical building of the church and the human body which both needs to be taken care of in order to please the Lord. Let us look at another aspect of the temple of God which the New Testament places emphasis on:

> Don't you know that you yourselves are God's temple and that God's Spirit lives in you? If anyone destroys God's temple, God will destroy him; for God's temple is sacred, and you are that temple (1 Corinthians 3:16 -17).

It is a privilege that our bodies can become the temple of the almighty God. Since a believer's life is for God, he or she must take good care of their lives. They cannot live anyhow without due reverence to God. But how can people prioritize their lives or body in order to please God? How can believers become a vessel of honour for God to use? St. Paul advice in 2 Timothy 2:20-22:

> In a large house there are articles not only of gold and silver, but also of wood and clay; some are for noble purposes and some for ignoble. If a man cleanses himself from the latter, he will be an instrument for noble purposes, made holy, useful to the Master and prepared to do any good work. Flee the evil desires of youth, and pursue righteousness, faith, love and peace, along with those who call on the Lord out of a pure heart.

We must get rid of anything that can contaminate us, and pursue righteousness, faith, love, and peace. This lifestyle will create the atmosphere for God to dwell and use us as vessels for noble purposes. For an unbeliever however, the outmost thing I will suggest in this book is for you to receive Christ as Lord and saviour, and be born again. The Lord himself will then lead you through the next line of actions. To be born again or to receive eternal life is the highest attainment in life. A born again person is a person born of heaven, because he or she has received the life of God which will grant that person access to heavenly blessings now and in the new world to come. Faith in Jesus Christ, repentance, baptism, and a desire to live for God are the fundamental requirements for a born again Christian's life style.

In this section we have looked at how certain places are sacred, and what people need to do when they come to such places. Do not desecrate a holy place by what you do or say. Humans beings become sacred or the temple of God when they allow the Spirit of God to live in them as they are born again or as they receive the new birth in Christ Jesus.

2. Certain Objects are Sacred

Ordinary objects or items such as stones, special formulated incense and oil, basins, utensils, garments become sacred upon the divine God declaring them Holy, especially when any of these objects have been consecrated for special use by God. For example, concerning the use of basins for the things of God, the instruction given in the Old Testament was that : 'the table and all its articles, the lamp stand and its accessories, the altar of incense, the altar of burnt offerings and all its utensils, and the basin with its stand. You shall consecrate them so they will be most holy, and whatever touches them will be holy' (Exodus 30:28-29).

Any object made Holy to the Lord should be treated with respect, care and of reverence for God. Do you know that specially formulated anointing perfumes are to be used on only God's priest in the Old Testament times? This is what God said:

> This is to be my sacred anointing oil for the generations to come. Do not pour it on men's bodies and do not make any oil with the same formula. It is sacred, and you are to consider it sacred. Whoever makes perfume like it and whoever puts it on anyone other than a priest must be cut off from his people (Exodus 30:31-33).

Sacred things should not be made for any common use. It is a great affront to God to jest with sacred things, and to make sport with his word and ordinances. We can learn something from what happened to Uzzah who was smitten for his irreverence in handling the ark of God, an object which represented the presence of God:

> When they came to the threshing floor of Nacon, Uzzah reached out and took hold of the ark of God, because the oxen stumbled. The LORD'S anger burned against Uzzah because of his irreverent act; therefore God struck him down and he died there beside the ark of God (2 Samuel 6:6-7).

A man called Uzzah died because he did not handle the Ark of God with respect. According to some Biblical commentators, the Ark of God was supposed to be carried and administered only by the Levites (Deuteronomy 31:25). This man, Uzzah was not a Levite, and was not consecrated to handle the Ark, hence his sudden tragedy. The Bible says David was afraid of the LORD that day and said; how can the ark of the LORD ever come to me? David was not willing to take the ark of the LORD to be with him in the City of David. Instead, he took it aside to the house of Obed-Edom the Gittite. The ark of the LORD remained in the house of Obed-Edom the Gittite for three months, and the LORD blessed him and his entire household. Now King David was told, The LORD has blessed the household of Obed-Edom and everything he has, because of the ark of God. So David went down and brought up the ark of God from the house of Obed-Edom to the City of David with rejoicing' (2 Samuel 6:9-12).

People who take very good care of sacred objects are indeed blessed. Make this one of your ambitions today. Take very good care of everything that belongs to God, you will be blessed. If you have dedicated your child to God or baptised your child to God, please take good care of that child because he or she is sacred unto the Lord and God will bless you richly for doing that.

In the New Testament, communion, offerings, the message of the Bible, servants of God, believers worship places are all sacred. In 1 Corinthians 11, the Bible says some people in the church at Corinth were partaken in the Holy Communion in an unworthy manner and so they became ill, weak and dead:

> Therefore, whoever eats the bread or drinks the cup of the Lord in an unworthy manner will be guilty of sinning against the body and blood of the Lord. A man ought to examine himself before he eats of the bread and drinks of the cup. For anyone who eats and drinks without recognizing the body of the Lord eats and drinks judgment on himself. That is why many among you are weak and sick, and a number of you have fallen asleep' (1 Corinthians 11:27-30).

Because the elements of the communion are holy, people should be careful when given the chance to partake in Holy Communion.

The Holy Communion is a shared meal between Christ and the church. Anything that has to do with the church of God is Holy and offers both blessings and curses depending on how worshippers attend to these things. In the same way, it is dangerous and fatal for people to use professions of the gospel of Christ to forward worldly interests.

In this section, we are looking at the fact that we have sacred places and sacred objects. King Solomon offers a very good advice:

> Guard your steps when you go to the house of God. Go near to listen rather than to offer the sacrifice of fools, who do not know that they do wrong. Do not be quick with your mouth; do not be hasty in your heart to utter anything before God. God is in heaven and you are on earth, so let your words be few (Ecclesiastes 5:1-2).

In conclusion, we ought to approach God with a solemn pause and preparation; and to express our inward reverence by a reverent behaviour in the worship of God, carefully avoiding everything that looks light or rude.

4.4 Certain Activities are Sacred

An activity is a behaviour or action of a particular kind for a particular purpose. It is obvious that all activities are not of the same importance.

> Just as you wouldn't leave the house without taking a shower, you shouldn't start the day without at least ten minutes of sacred practice: prayer, meditation, inspirational reading. **Marianne Williamson.**

Marianne Williamson says; prayer, meditation and inspirational reading of Bible or sacred texts should be given high priority before one starts his or her day. Prayer is a communication between you and God. So in prayer, you have the opportunity to ask God for strength and guidance for the day. Meditation takes the mind beyond the distractions and noise of the moment to a broader level of awareness that notices causes and patterns within events. In a meditative state, one can get beyond his or her anger.

It is a good practice to make time to meditate before you begin the day if you can. God can also speak to you through scripture reading. The psalmist says, 'Your word is a lamp to my feet and a light for my path' (Psalm 119:105). The word of God if properly interpreted and applied can provide answers to your problems. A ten minutes devotional reading every morning or at your own set time can nourish your soul and guide you for the day.

In this section, my main point is that some activities are more important than others but this must be seen within a particular context or situation. As an example, Luke reports what happened when Jesus visited Mary and Martha at home:

> As Jesus and his disciples were on their way, he came to a village where a woman named Martha opened her home to him. She had a sister called Mary, who sat at the Lord's feet listening to what he said. But Martha was distracted by all the preparations that had to be made. She came to him and asked, Lord, don't you care that my sister has left me to do the work by myself? Tell her to help me! Martha, Martha, the Lord answered, you are worried and upset about many things, but only one thing is needed. Mary has chosen what is better, and it will not be taken away from her (Luke 10:38-42).

In this incident, Jesus did not blame Martha for being concerned about household chores. He was only asking her to set her priorities on things above. Mary was listening to Jesus' teachings while Martha was preparing food. Physical food and the word of God are both important. But the word of God is more important especially during preaching or teaching time in the church or in a fellowship than physical food. Are you Mary or Martha?
Some church members even fall asleep while the pastor is preaching. That is a wrong priority. There is time for everything. Preaching time is not the time for sleeping. Please learn to pay attention in church throughout the service. Every aspect of the service is important.

You can receive miracle by just listening to the sermon attentively. Two separate accounts in the book of Acts attest to this fact.

> In Lystra, there sat a man crippled in his feet, who was lame from birth and had never walked. He listened to Paul as he was speaking. Paul looked directly at him, saw that he had faith to be healed and called out, stand up on your feet! At that, the man jumped up and began to walk (Acts 14:8-10).

Paul stopped his discourse when he saw that the cripple had faith to be healed. He saw an opportunity to extend the interest in his message. please pay careful attention during church service. Make every effort to concentrate on the service so that you can be blessed. Faith comes by hearing the word of God (Romans 10:17). In a different account Dr Luke tells us the following:

> On the first day of the week we came together to break bread. Paul spoke to the people and, because he intended to leave the next day, kept on talking until midnight. There were many lamps in the upstairs room where we were meeting. Seated in a window was a young man named Eutychus, who was sinking into a deep sleep as Paul talked on and on. When he was sound asleep, he fell to the ground from the third story and was picked up dead. Paul went down, threw himself on the young man and put his arms around him. "Don't be alarmed, he said. He's alive! Then he went upstairs again and broke bread and ate. After talking until daylight, he left (Acts 20:7-11).

Unfortunately, this man Eutychus was sleeping during the service and nearly spoilt the church service. But thanks be to God that the brethren were encouraged again when the man rose from death. Please don't sleep when you go to the church.

4.5 Protecting & respecting the sources of your blessings

What I intend to do in this section is to encourage people to learn to protect the sources of their blessings- sacred people or objects or places. If the source of your blessings is taken away, you may suffer without help. 'Keep a family cow healthy and enjoy delicious milk, cream, cheese and more!' Unfortunately, many believers treat the sources of their blessings with disrespect, contempt, or expose them to harm. Many people unfortunately destroy the very things which are meant to be a blessing to them. Proverbs 11:29 says 'He who brings trouble on his family will inherit only wind'. You may never benefit or gain anything good out of what you do not have regard for. Many married partners have destroyed their own families, through unfaithfulness, and lack of respect and commitment towards each other. Many parents have neglected their parental responsibilities towards their children, so these children could not bless their parents when they grew up. If you are a man and you want your wife to treat you with respect, love and kindness, then it is your duty to take good care of your family.

If you want your boss to treat you well, then you must also treat him or her well and vice versa. If you are employer and you want your employees to be faithful and hardworking then you must treat them well.

A child can easily destroy the very toys he or she is playing with and cry for new toys. Sadly, many people behave in the same manner. But why would people destroy or refuse to take good care of what is meant to be a blessing to them? There are many reasons! Sometimes people do that out of ignorance or lack of knowledge; sometimes they do so out of foolishness or childishness. St. Paul once said 'When I was a child, I talked like a child; I thought like a child, I reasoned like a child. When I became a man, I put childish ways behind me.[7] To put away childish things or thinking and embracing mature adulthood is not something that happens automatically with age. There must be a conscious decision making, to embrace mature adult lifestyles and act responsibly. Some decisions may be difficult to

---

[7] 1 Corinthians 13:11

follow through but the end is always good. So learn to protect the source of your blessings.

Protecting the name of God: You must love God, respect his name, and honour him because He is the Great God, the creator and our Father who art in heaven. Exodus 20:7 says 'You shall not misuse the name of the LORD your God, for the LORD will not hold anyone guiltless who misuses his name'. In Job 2:9-10, we see how a man called Job kept his integrity with God when Satan afflicted him with painful sores from the soles of his feet to the top of his head: 'His wife said to him, Are you still holding on to your integrity? Curse God and die! The man replied, You are talking like a foolish woman. Shall we accept good from God, and not trouble? In all this, Job did not sin in what he said'. Many people blame God and say many unkind words about him, when they are going through life challenges. This should not be so. Never say anything bad about God, respect your creator. Honour God and He will also glorify you. Remember, you will stand before Him one day on that judgment day.

The book of Job 42:12-17, tells us the beautiful end result of those who protect their integrity in God, no matter what they go through:

> The LORD blessed the latter part of Job's life more than the first. He had fourteen thousand sheep, six thousand camels, a thousand yoke of oxen and a thousand donkeys. And he also had seven sons and three daughters. The first daughter he named Jemimah, the second Keziah and the third Keren-Happuch. Nowhere in all the land were there found women as beautiful as Job's daughters, and their father granted them an inheritance along with their brothers. After this, Job lived a hundred and forty years; he saw his children and their children to the fourth generation. And so he died, old and full of years.

Job stands as the clearest Old Testament example of unfairness: an upright man, who suffered greatly, yet did not blame or curse God. Jesus stands as the New Testament example: a perfect man who suffered even more for the sins of the world; at the hands of the people He hoped to save. Both hint at a happy ending after all. What lesson have you learnt? Honor God and do not misuse his name.

Protecting the name of Jesus Christ your saviour

Jesus Christ is the saviour of the world (1 John 4:14). He is the source of eternal blessings to all who will believe in him. In John 14:13-14 Jesus says, 'I will do whatever you ask in my name, so that the Son may bring glory to the Father'. You may ask me for anything in my name, and I will do it'. You must therefore protect the name and integrity of Jesus Christ. Jesus says 'Whoever acknowledges me before men, I will also acknowledge him before my Father in heaven. But whoever disowns me before men, I will disown him before my Father in heaven (Matthew 10:23-33). He is the name above every name, cherish his name because prophetically 'God has exalted him to the highest place and has given him the name that is above every name, that at the mention of the name of Jesus every knee should bow, in heaven and on earth and under the earth, and every tongue confess that Jesus Christ is Lord, to the glory of God the Father (Philippians 2:8-11). A day is coming when both believers and unbelievers will bow down at the mentioning of the name Jesus. Believers will bow to Him in worship because He is their saviour and King while unbelievers will bow to Him in shame for refusing to accept Him as Lord during their life time. This will take place a time yet to come.

What else can you benefit from the name of Christ? There is power in his name, and you can receive answered prayer in his name. In John 14:13-14, Jesus says 'I tell you the truth, anyone who has faith in me will do what I have been doing. He will do even greater things than these, because I am going to the Father. And I will do whatever you ask in my name, so that the Son may bring glory to the Father. You may ask me for anything in my name, and I will do it'. Don't allow anyone to pollute your mind about Jesus Christ. Have faith in him, pray in his name, and it shall be granted.

Some people may say bad things about Jesus Christ please correct them and gently explain who Jesus Christ is to them. For example, tell them that Jesus is the saviour of the world (1 John 4:14). 1 Peter 3:15-17, offers helpful ways to protect and honor the name of Jesus. It says, 'in your hearts set apart Christ as Lord. Always be prepared to give an answer to everyone who asks you to give the reason for the hope that you have. But do this with gentleness and respect'.

Protecting your local church. Your local church is also a source of blessing to you. I am aware that one of the key elements of post-modernity[8] is 'individuality without belonging' or believing without belonging. This trend has affected many people's relationship with their local churches in many ways. For example, this has encouraged many people to consider church-going as a choice rather than a way of devotion to God. And so, in this section I will be encouraging us to be committed to a local church because of the many benefits. Some people are attracted to bigger and popular churches. Joining a bigger or a popular church doesn't make you great in the sight of God. In fact most people are only spectators in these bigger churches. Look for a church where you can really belong; where you can be discipled and nurtured to grow and become mature to serve God. And if you can get these opportunities in bigger churches, good! Smaller churches always need more hands than the bigger churches.

Let us discuss some of the benefits of belonging to a local church. When St. Peter was put in prison for preaching the gospel, it was his local church that prayed for his release (Acts 12:1-17). James 5:14-15 also says 'Is any one of you sick? He should call the elders of the church to pray over him and anoint him with oil in the name of the Lord. And the prayer offered in faith will make the sick person well; the Lord will raise him up. If he has sinned, he will be forgiven'. When you are sick, you have to inform your church leaders and they will pray for you for healing and you will be healed.

Sadly, many church members, out of ignorance and lack of respect for their leaders, do not do this when they are sick. Some church members prefer to call the television preacher for healing, than their church leaders but that is not how God has ordained it. Television or media preachers should be

---

[8]**Postmodernity** or the **postmodern** condition is the economic or cultural state or condition of western society which is said to exist after modernity. Some people argue that we are in postmodern world; others too are of the opinion that modernity and postmodernity are in co-existence.

there to evangelist and to bring new people to the Christian faith. Every true believe should belong to a local church. Many church members move from one church to another for help, this is a bad practice too. Stay in your local church and pray for it to be a Christ-centered church and God will meet you there at your point of need.

The local church is also a place where we can draw our spiritual strength. 1 Corinthians 12 describes the church, universal or local as a body with many different parts. In this text, the word of God gives a clever anatomy lesson, with a purpose. By comparing members of the church of Christ to parts of a human body, the Bible neatly explains two complementary truths the Corinthian church had failed to comprehend. Any part of a body, the writer says—such as an eye or a foot—makes a valuable contribution to the whole body. Whenever a single member is missing, the entire body suffers. To prevent the entire body from suffering, God removes unfaithful members from the church spiritually long before the person decides to leave the church so that their departure will not affect the church. St. John tells a church he wrote to this: 'They went out from us, but they did not really belong to us. For if they had belonged to us, they would have remained with us; but their going showed that none of them belonged to us (1 John 2:19).

St Paul continues his discussion on church membership in 1 Corinthians 12 saying that no member can survive if isolated from the rest of the church members. As a believer in the Lord, you need the church to survive spiritually because you are a part of the church. The body of Christ is the church. An eye alone is useless. An eyeless body can cope, but a bodiless eye is unimaginable. The most beautiful eyes in the world, when detached from a body, are lifeless and worthless. Eyes need a body that will bring them blood and receive their nerve impulses. In the same way, every church member needs the local church in order to be nourished. Once you allow Satan to deceive you to leave the church, you start dying spiritually. Leaving the church is like leaving the presence of God.

The church can be compared to the Garden of Eden. The church is the gathering of God's children- *(the Ecclesia)*. Psalm 1:5 says 'Therefore the wicked will not stand in the judgment, nor sinners in the assembly of the righteous'. Adam and Eve allowed themselves to be corrupted by Satan. This is one of the reasons why God drove Adam and Eve from the Garden of Eden. The wicked cannot survive in the assembly of the righteousness. Sinners are always welcomed to the house of God; a place where their sins could to be forgiven. There is difference between a sinner and a wicked person. We all sin because we are born sinners (Romans 3:23). A wicked person is someone who suppresses the truth, or who plans intentionally to do evil. Such a person will not be allowed in the gathering of God's people, unless he or she repents. There have been times when God had to drive certain people from the church because they were causing havoc.

Jesus always sees the house of God as the house of His Father; so should we. Praying for the church is one of the ways we can protect the church. We can pray for God's blessings as well, we can work to promote unity in the church. We need to engage in evangelism, so that we can fulfil our mandates as Christians, and, at the same time contribute to the numerical growth of the local church by witnessing Christ to people.

Protecting Your Leader- Pastor, Archbishop…

It is a wise thing to protect your primary leader, because he or she is a vessel God is using to bless you. You must also protect the other leaders in your church and even your church members. Many people are suffering, even in the church because they refused to protect someone God sent into their lives to bless them. Your destiny is somehow connected to other people. Let us briefly look at how king David's men protected him:

> Once again there was a battle between the Philistines and Israel. David went down with his men to fight against the Philistines, and he became exhausted. And Ishbi-Benob, one of the descendants of Rapha, whose bronze spearhead weighed three hundred shekels and who was armed with a new sword, said he would kill David. But Abishai son of Zeruiah came to David's rescue; he struck the Philistine down and killed him. Then David's men swore to him, saying, "Never again will you go out with us to battle, so that the lamp of Israel will not be extinguished (2 Samuel 21:15-17).

God blessed him and his descendants. In this text, David fainted, but he did not flee, and God sent help in the time of need. In spiritual conflicts, even strong saints sometimes wax faint; then Satan attacks them furiously; but those who stand their ground and resist him, shall be relieved and made more than conquerors. Protect your leader like the way David men cared for him. Do not be part of the people who speak ill of their leaders, and make every effort to correct any bad impression that anyone could have about your primary leaders. Do not also be ignorant of your leaders' fallibility. They are equally human like you and are also prone to mistakes. Pray for them and God will bless you in return.

Some people will watch for the leader to be destroyed without offering help. Some will even join in the attack against their leader just to destroy or assassinate his or her character. But when they are in trouble, they will pray to God for help. God may not answer the prayers of people who do not have love for the people God sent to help them.

Leading a church can be difficult sometimes. The overseer carries special anointing different from the other leaders of the church and because of this; the enemy is always attacking the leader. Because of this, he or she needs special protection. The enemy knows that if he can overcome the leader, it will be easier for him to overcome and scatter the church members back to the world. 'Strike the shepherd, and the sheep of the flock will be scattered' (Matthew 26:31).The enemy can cause certain people to speak ill about the leader, especially when the overseer is pulling God's children from the enemy's camp. As a member of a local church, do all you can to protect and bless your pastor or overseer! It is to your benefit to have a strong and anointed leader. If you don't have a good leader, this can affect your Christian life in many ways.

In the book of Acts 16:16-23, Paul and Silas, were falsely accused, beaten, and jailed because they delivered someone from demonic possession. This is an example of what leaders go through on regular basis; false accusations, confrontations, attacks, imprisonment etc. In spite of all these challenges, the Lord's faithfulness has been assured. God is in control of their lives.

However, because they are human, and live among us, they will need our support in order to be able to go on with the work of the Lord. Like we said earlier, they will definitely need our prayers. Ephesians 6:19-20 states:

> Pray also for me, that whenever I open my mouth, words may be given me so that I will fearlessly make known the mystery of the gospel, for which I am an ambassador in chains. Pray that I may declare it fearlessly, as I should.

Always pray for your leaders so that utterances may be given to them from heaven to the entire church and also pray that they will preach the truth because truth sets people free from any bondage.

There are two more ways you can protect your leader or overseer. The first one is found in Psalm 105:15: 'Do not touch my anointed ones; do my prophets no harm'. Do not harm your church leader, or any other leader. God will discipline you. The second one is found in Galatians 6:6: 'anyone who receives instruction in the word he must share all good things with his instructor.' Learn to share material things with your leader because he is sharing spiritual blessings with you. The church in Philippi shared material things with the apostle Paul; this is an excerpt of the grace the apostle bestowed on that church:

> Moreover, as you Philippians know, in the early days of your acquaintance with the gospel, when I set out from Macedonia, not one church shared with me in the matter of giving and receiving, except you only; for even when I was in Thessalonica, you sent me aid again and again when I was in need. Not that I am looking for a gift, but I am looking for what may be credited to your account. I have received full payment and even more; I am amply supplied, now that I have received from Epaphroditus the gifts you sent. They are a fragrant offering, an acceptable sacrifice, pleasing to God. And my God will meet all your needs according to his glorious riches in Christ Jesus (Philippians 4:15-19).

Paul blessed the church members in Philippi for the gift they gave him. I personally love the apostle Paul because he worked so hard for the kingdom of God, planting churches, preaching and defending the gospel before hostile audiences, Shipwrecked, beaten, imprisoned. Paul had seen the down side of life. He has also known prosperity. Both, he suggests, offer temptations. But Paul discovered a secret for contentment in all situations: his deeply personal sense of living in Christ. In this, he found strength to handle anything. God richly blessed his soul.

Protecting other Leaders in the church: As we discussed in the previous section, the overseer carries special anointing for special kind of service. Because of this he needs special protection. In the same way, you must protect the other leaders in the church because they are serving you. Don't speak evil or gossip about them, but respect them, pray for them, and obey their instructions.

Protecting other church members: God has brought you together with other people in the church for mutual benefits. You and I have a duty to protect one another from backsliding, from harm, from failing in life, from the influence of bad people in and outside the church. We have a fundamental duty to protect and love one another in the church. God is the source of your blessings, but he does disseminate this blessing through what I call, the local agents. These local agents include your local church, your Senior Pastor and other Leaders, other church members, and your work mates. How do you protect them? Follow the way of love!

Chapter 5

Prioritizing your Spiritual, Social, & Material Capitals

Human beings are material, spiritual, and social beings, and therefore we need material, spiritual, and social help to enable us function well. In this chapter, we will be discussing how to prioritize our material, social, and spiritual capitals. All these are essential for the survival of the human race; individually and as a community. I am grateful to Danah Zohar and Ian Marshall for their discussions on the three capitals in their book, *Spiritual Capital: The wealth we can live by*. Some of their ideas are used in this chapter. They define wealth as 'that which we have access to that enhances the quality of life'. The word wealth itself comes from the old English word *welth*, meaning 'to be well'. But the dictionary's definition of wealth, reflecting the economized culture that has produced our modern dictionaries, emphasised first, 'a great quantity or stored money'. Our usual definition of capital follows from this, defining capital as the amount of money or goods that we possess. In this sense, I see what we call wealth or capital as very narrow and inadequate because we human beings are spiritual, social, and material, hence the need to extend what capital is to these areas of the human personality: spiritual, social, and material.

The meaning of what material capital should be is not difficult to define. Material capital is the physical wealth such as money, houses, land, possessions, etc. In this book, I define social capital as the strength, or the encouragement, or the love, or the inspiration we draw from our fellow human beings, or the human community to enhance our lives in order to achieve our God given potentials. Francis Fukuyama defines social capital as the ability of people to work together for common purposes in groups and in organizations. Zohar and Marshall define social capital as the wealth that makes our communities and organisation function effectively for the common good. They equally defined spiritual capital as the amount of spiritual knowledge and expertise available to an individual or a culture; where spiritual is taken to mean 'meaning, values, and fundamental purposes'. But this definition of what spiritual capital is is too narrow because their definition of spiritual capital has no connection with religion or any organised belief system, but purely in business context. But we will discuss this further later on.

My personal order of priority will be, the spiritual, the social, and then material capital, in that order. 'No other kind of capital really works without an underlying base of spiritual capital.'[9] But it can be sometimes fatal to view these three capitals in this order. There are times when food for the stomach is very important to the extent that prayer or the reading of the scripture cannot be a substitute. There are equally things that only prayer (a source of spiritual strength) can do. There are times too when meeting other people becomes more important than food for the stomach. And so, what is needed is a balanced priority of all these three capitals.

Do you know that in order for God to get humanity back to Himself in relationship, He became human Himself in the person of His son Jesus Christ? This is what Christians call 'the doctrine of the incarnation of Christ'. John 1:14 says, 'The Word became flesh and made His dwelling among us. We have seen His glory, the glory of the One and only, who came from the Father, full of grace and truth'. The book of Hebrews goes further than any other New Testament book in explaining Jesus' human nature. Why was it so important that Jesus share our humanity? Hebrews stresses three reasons: first so that, in dying, He could free us from the power of death (Hebrews 2:14-15); secondly, so that, by becoming the final sacrifice for our sins, Jesus could reconcile us to God (Hebrews 5:8-9); and thirdly so that, in experiencing temptation, Jesus can better help us with our own temptations (Hebrews 2:18). And so the material world is important as the incarnation of Christ helps us to understand. In order of priority, as discussed earlier,

---

[9] *Spiritual capital* by Danah & Ian, page 10

spiritual capital comes first, social capital comes second, and then followed by material capital.

Sometimes, God can favour you with material capital before blessing you with spiritual capital or vice versa. Some people can become materially wealthy before they come to the faith in Jesus Christ for their salvation or before they begin to seek God. Others too, can be spiritually blessed before they are blessed materially. The lesson here is that, whichever comes first either spiritual capital, material capital or social capital, you must receive it, else you may miss the opportunity. It is possible that a young lady or a young man can meet someone they can settle down with, but may not have secured their dream job or dream profession yet. In such a situation, it is advisable to settle down in marriage or at least engage the person first before you lose him or her. The rest of the capitals will come at the appropriate time. There can also be a situation whereby one will have the opportunity to develop their spiritual capital first before they become materially wealthy.

We develop our spiritual capital by spending more time to pray, in meditation, read the scriptures, attend church service, and give alms to the poor, witness Christ and making every effort to live a holy life, acceptable before God.

5.1 God is the provider of all capitals

Where should people resource their spiritual capital and social capital? This is the question most writers on these subjects tend to avoid. For example, Danah Zohar's definition above is very helpful for our discussion in this chapter. But what is lacking in her definition in my opinion, is the source of this capital. From where should people resource their spiritual capital? The original source of all capital is God, the creator of the universe. This scriptural quotation summarises my main argument:

> For we brought nothing into this world, and it is certain we can carry nothing out of it (1 Timothy 6:7).

No human being brought anything into this world and no human being can take anything out of this world when the soul separates from the body at death. Secondly, even during our life time on this earth, whatever everyone has in this world was passed on to him or her or acquired. Because of this, the apostle Paul could say 'For what I received from the Lord, I passed on to you as of first importance: that Christ died for our sins according to the Scriptures, that He was buried, that He was raised on the third day according to the Scriptures (1 Corinthians 15:3-4).

This text and other scriptural references tell us that someone else brought what we see in this world into being at least in it raw material form. Who then, is the source of all things? The answer is God! The Bible begins with words that have become famous, 'In the beginning God created the heavens and the earth (Genesis 1:1). By the seventh day God had finished the work He had been doing; so on the seventh day He rested from all His work. And God blessed the seventh day and made it holy, because on it He rested from all the work of creating that He had done (Genesis 2:1-3). God, like an artist, fashioned a universe including human life.

Where did humans come from? A biology teacher displays a chart showing six animals. At one end is an ape standing upright, its hands swinging below its knees. At the other end, a rather hairy, stooped man in skins. These are the stages of human evolution, over a period of several million years, the teacher declares. One agonized student shoots up his hand. I believe in the Bible, he stammers, that God made the earth and that the first man was Adam'. 'But for Adam (the first man) no suitable helper was found. So the LORD God caused the man to fall into a deep sleep; and while he was sleeping, He took one of the man's ribs and closed up the place with flesh. Then the LORD God made a woman from the rib He had taken out of the man, and He brought her to the man. The man said, "This is now bone of my bones and flesh of my flesh; she shall be called 'woman,' for she was taken out of man' (Genesis 2:20-23).

Where did humans come from? Above all else, the book of Genesis 2:7 tells us that 'the LORD God formed the man from the dust of the ground and breathed into his nostrils the breath of life, and the man became a living being'. But how can we grasp the grandeur of this? First, the truth is, the Bible does not adequately explain everything about creation and God. We will always have questions about creation and God, but at least we are reminded of the fact that God created us, something St. Paul did when he gave a remarkable speech to a gathering of philosophers and thinkers in the sophisticated university city of Athens (Acts 17:16-34). The knowledge about creation itself should lead us to thank God, for His provision and to enjoy what He has given us: 'For everything God created is good and nothing is to be rejected if it is received with thanksgiving because it is consecrated by the word of God and prayer' (1 Timothy 4: 4-5).

The knowledge of God known through creation is what we called natural theology. But relying on natural theology alone can lead us to become idol worshipers like the Athenians. The ancients used to say, 'It is easier to find a god than a man in Athens'. And so St. Paul soon began to reveal to the Athenians the true God who alone deserves to be worshipped by all people. True knowledge about God comes to us through what is called special revelation. Special revelation, as contained in the Holy Bible tells us about God's commandments to help us worship Him acceptably (2 Tim 3:16-17). Faith in the true God comes from His word (Romans 10:17). But trying to know God through the written text alone in the Bible without union with Him can lead to hypocrisy, like the Pharisees in Jesus' days (Matthew 23:1-3). Many people are hypocrites because they only read the Bible; they do not do what the Bible says.

One of the essences of the message in the Bible is to lead us to union with God or Christ (John 5:39-40; John 20:30-31). And this union with God or what I call 'Direct Personal Communion with God' becomes possible as we practice what the Bible says, not just reading it. The Bible records that 'And the scripture was fulfilled that says, Abraham believed God, and it was credited to him as righteousness; and he was called God's friend' (James 2:23). Abraham was an idol worshiper (Joshua 24:2-4) but God called him to a new life. He later earned a status as God's friend (Isaiah 41:8) and the father of faith. I challenge you to become a friend of God, like this great man Abraham.

Back to our original question, who then, is the source of all our capitals? Psalm 145:16 says 'You [God] open your hand and satisfy the desire of every living thing'. Look at the birds of the air says Jesus in Matthew 6:26, 'they do not sow, nor reap nor gather into barns, and yet your heavenly Father feeds them. Are you not worth much more than they'? God also reminds his people the following:

> You may say to yourself, my power and the strength of my hands have produced this wealth for me. But remember the LORD your God, for it is He who gives you the ability to produce wealth, and so confirms his (His) covenant, which he swore to your forefathers, as it is today(Deuteronomy 8:18-19).

Here, there is a renewed emphasis on the writer's chief principle that Jehovah is the author of the every blessing. When men possess large estates, or are engaged in profitable business, they find the temptation to pride themselves and forget their God. In everything, we must give thanks to God and remember that He is the source of everything we have, including our ability to produce either wealth (material capital) or offspring (social capital) or to receive the gift of salvation (spiritual capital).

'For we brought nothing into the world, and we can take nothing out of it'. This verse is quoted by Polycarp[10], in his letter to the Philippians, written early in the second century. Such reference shows that this Epistle was known and treasured in the Christian Church even at that early date, 'For we brought nothing into this world'. A sentiment very similar to this occurs in the book of Job 1:21:

> Naked I came out of my mother's womb, and naked shall I return thither: the LORD gave, and the LORD has taken away; blessed be the name of the LORD (Job 1:21).

---

[10] Polycarp was a 2nd-century Christian bishop of Smyrna. According to the Martyrdom of Polycarp he died a martyr, bound and burned at the stake, then stabbed when the fire failed to touch him.

All that we have is a gift from God, and He is able to recall them if He so wishes. We could take a lesson from the attitude of a man called Job. The Bible says, 'in all this, Job did not sin by charging God with wrong doing' (Job, 1:22). May the Lord help us to always remember this truth that all we have and will ever have come from Him. We came into this world naked, with nothing, and we will return naked, with nothing to where we came from. This alone should humble us to seek and to worship the great God who made us. I have discussed how God provides us with spiritual, social, and material capitals in the next three sections.

5.2 Spiritual Capital

There are many definitions of what spiritual capital is. As already mentioned, we will be working beyond Zohar and Marshal's definition. Their definition posits spiritual capital as the amount of spiritual knowledge and expertise available to an individual or a culture, where spiritual is taken to mean 'meaning, values, and fundamental purposes'. The word spiritual comes originally from the Latin *spiritus,* which means 'that which gives life or vitality to a system'. Jesus Christ says, 'God is spirit, and his worshipers must worship in spirit and in truth' (John 4:24).

What are some of the examples of spiritual capital?

In recent times, when people say they are spiritual, they mean different things. The common definition of what it means to be spiritual in a secular sense is the search for meaning, values, and purpose. Where can people even find these meaning, values and purpose in life? But spiritual capital is more than meanings, values, and purpose. Spiritual capital is the strength or the capital we get from the *spiritus* in order to spend or invest. The meaning of *spiritus* (spirit) is that which gives life or vitality to a system, or a human being. John 4:24 tells us that 'God is Spirit'. From this understanding, we can therefore say that spiritual capital is the strength or the capital we get from the Spirit of God. With this definition in mind, we have unlimited kinds of spiritual capital at our disposal. For those who lack self-control, love, and those who are timid, the Bible says 'For God did not give us a spirit of timidity, but a spirit of power, of love and of self-discipline (2 Timothy 2:1). The capital or strength we can gain from the Spirit of God is limitless. But be warned, Satan can also give false spirit!

Galatians 5:22-24 further, tells us the moral result which the Spirit of God or the Holy Spirit brings about as His fruit. The fruit of the Spirit is love, joy, peace, patience, kindness, goodness, faithfulness, gentleness and self-control. Against such things there is no law. Those who belong to Christ Jesus have crucified the sinful nature with its passions and desires'. It is perhaps not too artificial to point out that we have here three triads of which the first describes the life of the Spirit in its deepest secret; the second, the same life in its manifestations to men; and the third, that life in relation to the difficulties of the world, and of ourselves.

The first of these three triads includes love, joy, and peace, and it is not putting too great a strain on the words to point out that the source of all three lies in the Christian relation to God. The second triad is long-suffering, kindness, goodness. All these three obviously refer to the spiritual life and its manifestations to other people. The first of them, long-suffering, describes the attitude of patience endurance towards inflictors or enemies. If we come forth from the blessed fellowship with God, where love, joy, and peace reign unbroken, and are met with a cold gust of indifference or with an icy wind of hate. Answer a fool according to his folly (Proverbs, 26:5), but it takes a wise and a good man to overcome evil with good. It takes two to make a quarrel, and no man living under the influence of the Spirit of God can be one of such a pair.

The third triad- faithfulness, meekness, and temperance--seems to point to the world in which the Christian life is to be lived as a scene of difficulties and oppositions. Christian life is to manifest itself in the faithful discharge of all duties and the honest handling of all things committed to it. Meekness even more distinctly contemplates a condition of things which is contrary to the Christian life, and points to a submissiveness of spirit which does not lift itself up against oppositions, but bends like a reed before the storm. The last member of the triad--temperance-points to the difficulties which the spiritual life is apt to meet with in the natural passions and desires, and insists upon the fact that conflict and rigid and habitual self-control are sure to be marks of that life. People who lack self-control should seek more of this spiritual capital from God. All these can be obtained from God who gives his spirit alongside other blessings to us only if we will ask and believe (James 1:5-8).

There is one more kind of spiritual capital we can receive from God and that is spiritual gift or gifts for service. I Corinthians 12:1-11 summarises these as follows:

> Now about spiritual gifts, brothers, I do not want you to be ignorant. You know that when you were pagans, somehow or other you were influenced and led astray to mute idols. Therefore I tell you that no one who is speaking by the Spirit of God says, Jesus be cursed, and no one can say, Jesus is Lord, except by the Holy Spirit. There are different kinds of gifts, but the same Spirit. There are different kinds of service, but the same Lord. There are different kinds of working, but the same God works all of them in all men. Now to each one the manifestation of the Spirit is given for the common good. To one there is given through the Spirit the message of wisdom, to another the message of knowledge by means of the same Spirit, to another faith by the same Spirit, to another gifts of healing by that one Spirit, to another miraculous powers, to another prophecy, to another distinguishing between spirits, to another speaking in different kinds of tongues, and to still another the interpretation of tongues. All these are the work of one and the same Spirit, and He gives them to each one, just as He determines.

ource is the same. The confession of Christ as Lord is the true evidence that one has the Spirit of God. Spiritual gifts are extraordinarily powerful gifts bestowed upon Christians, to convince unbelievers, and to spread the gospel. Gifts and grace are two different things even though they are both freely given by God. But where grace is given, it is for the salvation of those who have it. Gifts are for the service to God and others.

When we turn to God for our spiritual capital (that which can give us life), we do not only get meaning, values and purpose, but we also get more than we expect; we get eternal life as well. This is one of the reasons I will argue that we all need to turn to God in repentance and make his service a priority. Those who have come to the Lord should share their experience with those who have not heard the gospel at all. Many people including some Christians shy away from acknowledging that God is the giver of life for various reasons.

This rejection of God as the source of spiritual capital can take place at different levels. First, people may use things from God, yet deny that He is the source of their life. Second, some people will acknowledge God, seek His blessings, but later forget to show appreciation to God when things are going on well. Thirdly, some people out of ignorance or rebelliousness have decided to believe that there is no God at all. The danger and consequences of denying the existence of God will be discussed further later in this chapter. However, it is important to know that there is a God who created the heavens and the earth; He is the giver of life and the source of all capital. We cannot talk about spiritual things without mentioning God. It is like having a discussion about the sea and being hesitant to mention water.

Fundamentally, spirituality or spiritual capital or spiritual intelligence all have something to do with the creator of the universe. This is because God is spirit (John 4:23-24) and He Himself gives all people life and breath and everything else, 'for in Him we live and move and have our being.' As some of your own poets have said, 'we are His offspring (Acts 17:28). The power for every act and sensation and thought comes from Him. Although Satan can also give people counterfeit power.

When Jesus was reading His manifesto in Nazareth, He did not fail to disclose the source of His strength. This is what He said:

> The Spirit of the Lord is on me, because He has anointed me to preach good news to the poor. He has sent me to proclaim freedom for the prisoners and recovery of sight for the blind, to release the oppressed, to proclaim the year of the Lord's favor (Luke 4:18-19).

The historical meaning is that: He, the Messiah, is inspired and ordained by God to announce to the deeply unfortunate people in their banishment that their liberation from captivity, and the blessed future of the restored and glorified theocracy that shall follow thereupon. The fulfilment of this scripture, i.e. the realization of their theocratic idea, came to pass in Christ and His ministry. The coming of the Spirit of God upon Jesus Christ at His baptism was the 'unction from the Holy One' (1 John 2:20) which confirmed His role as the Christ, the true anointed of the Lord. In the same way, it is the coming of the Spirit from the Father upon us, that will make us little Christ, His sons and daughters (Romans 8:14-17).

God gave His only begotten Son to the world, so that we might receive eternal life (John 3:16). And for the Son to be able to accomplish the task of saving humanity from sin and people from the grip of Satan, the Father had to pour His Spirit upon the Son.

The proof of this willingness of God is first the given to us of His only begotten Son as a sacrifice for our sins. But in order to receive certain things from God, one needs to prepare him or herself.

Preparing to receive spiritual capital

Sometimes, it is easier to get material capital and social capital, but to receive the true spiritual capital from God requires preparation. Those who desire to receive spiritual capital are encouraged to prepare themselves to receive from Him because sometimes God does not give His precious things to people who are double minded or people who are not prepared. Secondly, He does not give his precious resources, blessings or sacred gifts to people who are unable to handle it. A double minded person for example cannot receive from God.

> But when he asks, he must believe and not doubt, because he who doubts is like a wave of the sea, blown and tossed by the wind. That man should not think he will receive anything from the Lord; he is a double-minded man, unstable in all he does (James 1:6-8).

This 'doubting' is the halting between belief and unbelief, with inclination towards the latter. But it may be asked by someone, whence and how is an unhesitating faith to be gained? And the reply to this will solve all similar questions: faith, in its first sense, is the direct gift of God (Ephesians 2:8); but it must be tended and used with love and zeal, or its precious faculties will soon be gone. In the hour of some besetting thought of unbelief 'the shield of faith' will quench all the fiery darts of the wicked' (Ephesians 6:16), but that shield must be lifted up, as it were, in an act of faith. Assuming the enemy has wounded you, and you begin to doubt the faithfulness of God, what should you do? Let the battle-hymn of the Christian make quick answer, 'I believe in God' and often, with that very effort, the assault will cease for awhile. So, it is important not to doubt if you want to receive something from God. This is a requirement.

Let us look at the next spiritual requirement in order to receive sacred things from God:

> Do not give dogs what is sacred; do not throw your pearls to pigs. If you do, they may trample them under their feet, and turn and tear you to pieces (Matthew 7:6).

What is it that is very dear to you? Those things could be your pearls. In this text pearls are used to denote the doctrines of the gospel. 'Dogs' signify people who spurn, oppose, and abuse that doctrine; people of special sourness and malignity of temper, who meet it, like growling and quarrelsome curs. Swine denote those who would trample the precepts underfoot; people of impurity of life; those who are corrupt, polluted, profane, obscene, and sensual; those who would not know the value of the gospel, and who would tread it down as swine would pearls. The meaning of this proverb, then, is, do not offer your doctrine to those violent and abusive people who would growl and curse you; nor to those especially debased and profligate who would not see its value, but would trample it down, and would abuse you.

Pearls of life: Those things that are of value to you could be regarded as your pearls. Your pearls could be your heart, money, advice, property or anything that is dear to you. Please test whoever you want to entrust something precious into their care else you may end up casting your pearls before swine. As a woman, you must give your love and heart only to a man who will respect you in a relationship leading to marriage. The same advice applies to men. Many people in relationships have suffered broken hearts and disappointments because they gave their love and heart to the wrong person.

Give your body to a man or a woman who is qualified to take care of it. But give your soul, body, and spirit to God, because He is the only one who can take good care of it. 1 Peter 3:5 states, 'for you were like sheep going astray, but now you have returned to the Shepherd and Overseer of your souls'. Undoubtedly, the shepherd is Jesus Christ. Jesus says 'I am the good shepherd. The good shepherd lays down his life for the sheep' (John 10:11). Unlike modern-day shepherds, who use dogs to drive their flocks, Palestinian shepherds in Jesus' day walked ahead, calling the sheep to follow. Only a familiar voice would make them come.

In the Old Testament, God was called the 'Shepherd of Israel' (Psalm 80:1), and God's appointed leaders were often referred to as shepherds as well. In claiming to be the good shepherd, Jesus was asserting his leadership over a flock He was willing to die for. An image, something like this, must have filled the minds of Jesus' listeners as He described a good shepherd who 'lays down his life for his sheep' (John 10:11). Nothing—not even ravaging wolves or thieves would come between the good shepherd and his sheep. He would die to protect them. Indeed Jesus died for our sins:

> For what I received I passed on to you as of first importance : that Christ died for our sins according to the Scriptures, that he was buried, that he was raised on the third day according to the Scriptures (1 Corinthians 15:3-4).

I will encourage you to make this Jesus Christ your Lord and saviour so that He can be the shepherd of your soul. All authority in heaven and on earth has been given to Jesus Christ (Matthew 28:18). Many people are ignorant of spiritual things. You see, there are many bad people out there. These people can sacrifice your soul for power, fame, or monetary gain if you are not protected spiritually. There are also, people with witchcraft spirit who cast spells on people (Micah 5:12). These are all spiritual things. But many people do not know all this. They are only concerned about their physical body and material possessions. They neglect their soul and spirit. Your spirit and soul are very precious, entrust them to Jesus' care.

'Do not give to dogs what is sacred'. The doctrines of the gospel of Jesus Christ are some of the sacred things which should only be given to people who will respect it. Church leadership is another example of 'pearls' in the Kingdom of God and only born again matured well tested believers should be appointed to serve in such capacity. It is a mistake to appoint the wrong people into position of leadership in the church. They will not be helpful at all to the church. A leader 'must first be tested; and then if there is nothing against them, let them serve as deacons' (1 Timothy 3:10). Please test whoever you want to entrust something sacred into their care else you may end up giving sacred things to wrong the people.

Putting the wrong people into Christian leadership role is like putting Sanballat and Tobiah in the store room of a project to build the house of God. Sanballat and Tobiah were some of the adversaries Nehemiah had to contend with in rebuilding the walls of Jerusalem. When Sanballat, Tobiah and Geshem heard about Nehemiah's plans to rebuild the Jerusalem wall, they were at first grieved. When they saw that Nehemiah was executing his vision, they laughed him to scorn, despised the builders and accused them of rebelling against the king (see Nehemiah. 2:19). They oppose the work of God because they were unlawful leaders among God's people. Both of these men were connected to the Israelites through unlawful marriages (Nehemiah 6:18; 13:28). In the same way, any church leader who is not a true follower of Christ will oppose the work of God unnecessarily.

. Any time you set out to do something for God, you will find enemy opposition. The kingdom of God is not like human democratic government where we have a ruling party and opposition party. Jesus said 'Whoever is not with me is against me, and whoever does not gather with me scatters' (Matthew 12:30). So how do you handle such oppositions in your church or team? Do what Nehemiah did:

> Nehemiah's answer: The God of heaven, He will prosper us; therefore we His servants will arise and build: but ye have no portion, nor right, nor memorial, in Jerusalem (Nehemiah. 2:18).

If you are a leader or a visionary, please do not shrink back from confronting this spirit of Sanballat with the truth of God's Word. If you are confident in what God has called you to do, stand and build despite the scorners, despisers and accusers. And do not give them the right to build alongside you—or to speak into the work.

I think everyone has the tendency to act like Sanballat and Tobiah, and so there is the need for us to be careful. Sometimes we become opposition members when what is going on in the church or in the team does not favour us. If you think something is wrong or something is not in order in your church or team or workplace or even in your family, please find a peaceful means to discuss it. Do not create a scene or look for people to support your opposing stand. Such attitude can easily break the unity of the church or the team or the family. And the Lord may hold you guilty.

We have been discussing the importance of not 'given what is sacred to 'dogs', else they may trample upon it and tear you into pieces. We have just looked at the importance of this in Christian leadership in particular. When James and John asked Jesus to grant them the privilege 'to sit at his left and right in his glory', Jesus replied with the following words:

> You will drink the cup I drink and be baptized with the baptism I am baptized with, but to sit at my right or left is not for me to grant. These places belong to those for whom they have been prepared (Mark 10: 35-40).

Sacred things are given to those whom they have been prepared, not just anybody. I think the same principles can be applied in every aspect of life. But the question is; how does one prepare to receive spiritual capital? Repentance and showing respect for the things of God are some of the ways to prepare to receive from God. Allow yourself to be trained and tested. Many people desire certain sacred things, yet they are not ready to be trained for it. I have discussed the subject of prioritising sacred things earlier on in this book.

In this section, we have been discussing what spiritual capital is and how to obtain it. As Danah Zohar has rightly observed, 'Spiritual capital nourishes and sustains the human spirit.

5.3 Social Capital

I define social capital in this book as the strength, encouragement, love, or the inspiration we draw from our fellow human beings to enhance our lives in order to achieve our God given potentials. Francis Fukuyama defines social capital as the ability of people to work together for common purposes in groups and in organizations. Danah Zohar and Ian Marshall define social capital as the wealth that makes our communities and organisation functions effectively for the common good.

Many at times, the source of social capital for the individual is often overlooked and much emphasis is placed upon the individual's ability to make a contribution to the organisation or to the wider society. The result of this tendency is that many people feel increasingly, sapped, depressed, frustrated, and less effective because they do not even know where to turn to in order to be refreshed. In talking about social capital in this book, I am more interested in the source of this capital for the individual to function effectively whereas the other definitions we have referred to are more concerned about the individual's contribution towards the organisation or the society. If the individual is okay, he or she can be effective in any situation or role. Carl Jung, the distinguished analyst who took psychology beyond Freudian once said:

> If things go wrong in the world, this is because something is wrong with the individual, because something is wrong with me. Therefore if I am sensible, I shall put myself right first… in the last analysis, the essential thing is the life of the individual.

The individual make up the society. If the individual is okay, it is possible that the society will function well. The welfare of the society to some extent depends on the wellbeing of the individuals who make it up. When a society becomes corrupt, it is precisely because the individuals are corrupt. If a relationship breaks down, it is because there is something not okay with either one or the two or more of the members involved in that relationship. The prophet Isaiah in declaring God's word to the people concerning the devastation of the earth says:

> The earth is defiled by its people; they have disobeyed the laws, violated the statutes and broken the everlasting covenant. Therefore a curse consumes the earth; its people must bear their guilt. Therefore the earth's inhabitants are burned up, and very few are left (Isaiah 24:5-6).

The earth is defiled under the inhabitants thereof — by the wickedness of its people. Here we have the causes of the divine judgment upon the land: because they have transgressed the laws — the laws of God revealed to them. If the individual is okay, it is likely that they will not defile the earth. But the problem is that, we are sinners, imperfect beings, with the tendency to even destroy ourselves. If we can be endowed with some kind of capital, or help to guide us, and to make us better people, then there is hope, and God may relent in punishing us.

In the sections which follow, we will be discussing the importance, and sources of social capital, as well as how we can build healthy relationships.

The importance and sources of our social capital

Do you know that God sets the lonely in Families? Psalm 68:6; says 'God sets the lonely in families, He leads out the prisoners with singing; but the rebellious live in a sun-scorched land'. Genesis 2:18 says 'And the LORD God said, It is not good that the man should be alone; I will make him a help mate for him. The main purpose of social capital is to draw and share strength, support, love, and inspiration, with each other, and the community. There are times where we misunderstand, and abuse each other. These happenings go a long way to reiterate our human imperfections, and need to trust God for our day to day endeavours. Whereas God's original purpose is for us to take advantage of our interconnectedness to create a better world, our human fallibility rather deprives us from taking good advantage of this opportunity. If the purpose of something is unknown, abuse is inevitable. However, as the saying goes; 'to err is human'. It is the human that makes such mistake, not the God who created them. Besides our human fallibility, our lack of purpose and Satan's manipulations can also make us to abuse relationships.

Social capital as we have defined earlier enables as to draw and share our strength, love and inspiration from other individuals and the community at large; to help us to achieve our God given potentials on earth. God is the friend of the orphan and the widow, the outcast, the wanderer, and the homeless. But most importantly, He has an unconditional and undying love for us as His creatures. He is the friend to those who have no friends, father to the fatherless, and his whole creation. He is benevolent, kind, and promise to be with us through all the changing times if we remain faithful to Him.

The family is also appointed by Him to take on this role among us in human form. It is to provide comfort, relationship, and the protection that we need to as human beings in a chaotic yet interconnected world. Nothing more clearly explains the wisdom of God than the arrangement by which people, instead of being solitary wanderers on the face of the earth, with nothing to bind them in sympathy, in love, and in interest to each other, are grouped together into families. He gives children to those who are childless, and increases their families. Mankind is created as a material, spiritual, and as social being. Our full powers cannot be developed by physical and mental work alone; neither can our moral being by itself be disciplined in solitude. Our faculties and character require that it is to be expanded and beautified through it interactions and interconnectedness to family and other creatures.

The early hunter-gatherer societies required that individuals are able to hunt successfully to survive. Whereas there were individuals who were very astute in what they do, the individualist nature of the society made it difficult for survival in that era. God did not create us to be an island, but for us to belong to one another. Any human being who isolates himself or herself can die of loneliness. There are several instances in the scriptures that exemplified this. As already mentioned, when God created the first man, He said, 'It is not good for the man to be alone. I will make a helper suitable for him '(Genesis 2:18). When Moses complained to the Lord that he couldn't (could not) embark on his mission alone, his brother Aaron was sent to help and support him (Exodus 4:14). King Solomon says 'two are better than one, because they have a good return for their labour: If either of them falls down, one can help the other up. But pity anyone who falls and has no one to help them up. Also, if two lie down together, they will keep warm. But how can one keep warm alone? Though one may be overpowered, two can defend themselves. A cord of three strands is not quickly broken' (Ecclesiastes 4:9-12).

These references show that we have been created to belong, to draw strength, love, inspiration, anointing, and encouragement from each other. We can obtain social capital from the kinds of relationship we build in our families, communities, churches, and organisations. The trust we have for one another, the extent to which we fulfil our responsibilities to one another and the community, the amount of health and literacy we achieve through our common efforts, and the extent to which we are free from crime. All these can be a source of social capital, which we can harness in our service to God and our fellow human beings.

Food for thought: God did not give Adam a wife, for the couple to abandon Him, but that they both could celebrate their life with Him and to continue working together in His Kingdom. In the same way, in any human relationship you may find yourself, always remember that God is the unseen party in that relationship; ensure that the relationship gives glory to Him.

5.4 Guidelines to build healthy and beneficial relationships

As already discussed, the main purpose of any relationship is to draw strength, love, inspiration, and encouragement from each other in order to pursue our dreams, and ultimately serve God in our generation (Ecclesiastes 4: 9-12). But sometimes, we murder our own relationships by our attitudes; we fight and disagree with the very people sent to be a blessing to us. Galatians 5:15 says: 'If you keep on biting and devouring each other, watch out or you will be destroyed by each other'.

In view of this, the aim of this section is to look at how we can build healthy and beneficial relationships. Sometimes because of past bitter experiences with someone, many people have recoiled; some too are trying as much as possible to stay away from other people. The truth is that every human being is a social being, material being and spiritual being; no one is an island. For example, the fact that you are alone in your room or somewhere alone reading this book or watching television does not mean you are alone; you are interacting with someone's ideas, other aspects of creation or philosophy or even God Himself. Even, regarding prayer, there is nothing like private prayer. Because when you pray, depending on your religion, you are communicating with God in the name of Jesus Christ His son, and you do this through the help of the Holy Spirit. Here, you are engaging with the Trinity this process. Because of these and other reasons, it is important that you learn how to build healthy and beneficial relationships. We will look at six helpful guidelines that can help us do this.

1. **Learn to establish agreement(s)**

We are all different; we have different opinions, levels of comprehension, desires, dreams, and ways of life. In order to build a healthy relationship with other people, it may be necessary to learn to establish agreement of the terms of the relationship, formally or informally. Amos 3:3 says 'Do two walk together unless they have agreed to do so? Marriage couples should sit down and plan, or workout a framework within which to operate. This agreement is sometimes called covenant which is, usually formal, between two or more persons to do something or not do something. In the agreement, if possible, each party should make clear their likes and dislikes.

The same principle is needed in any form of relationship. For example, the military service is a covenant between a soldier and his commander, serving the interest of the nation. This is how God works. He always establishes an agreement or covenant with his people. Biblically, covenant is the conditional promises made to humanity by God, as revealed in Scripture. The Old Testament covenant or agreement is between God and the ancient Israelites as a point of contact, in which God promised to protect them (and others) if they kept His law and remained faithful to Him.

In the New Testament, God has promised to bless and save anyone who will believe in His son Jesus Christ, repent of their sins, be baptised, and aim to live a godly life (see John 3:36; Mark 16:15-18). We can learn something from how God the Father, the Son, and the Holy Spirit work together in unity. Jesus says' I and my Father are one (John 10:30). In John 5:19-20, Jesus says:

> I tell you the truth, the Son can do nothing by himself; he can do only what he sees his Father doing, because whatever the Father does the Son also does. For the Father loves the Son and shows him (Him) all He does. Yes, to your amazement he He will show him even greater things than these.

Jesus does what He sees the Father doing. And the Father continues to show the son what he does. Agreement is doing what two or more people have agreed to do. Establishing agreement can help build a healthy and beneficial relationship.

2. Do not fight people: Do not gossip or slander people

It is a mistake to fight people who come your way; they may be your guiding angels. Please, make the conscious effort not to fight unnecessarily with anyone who comes your way. Galatians 5:15 says; 'If you keep on biting and devouring each other, watch out or you will be destroyed by each other'. Husband and wife should not fight each other. Managers and their employees should not fight each other. Church members and their leaders should be at peace with each other. Family members should not fight each other.

Gossip and slandering is another negative vibe that destroys beautiful relationships. Proverbs 20:19 says 'gossip betrays a confidence; avoid a man who talks too much'. Proverbs 11:13 says 'gossip betrays confidence, but a trustworthy man keeps a secret. So, how can you become a good friend? The Old Testament puts great emphasis on close family relationships. Surprisingly, King Solomon in Proverbs rates a good friend even higher, for he or she 'sticks closer than a brother (Proverbs 18:24). Fair-weather friends are common (Proverbs 14:20) and the wrong kind of companions will bring you trouble. But a true friend loves you at all times, even when things are bad.

3. Be a peace Maker: live in peace with everyone

Romans 12:16-21, offers us a good advice on how we can be peace makers, even with those who hate us and the rewards we will get for living in harmony with everyone:

> Live in harmony with one another. Do not be proud, but be willing to associate with people of low position. Do not be conceited. Do not repay anyone evil for evil. Be careful to do what is right in the eyes of everybody. If it is possible, as far as it depends on you, live at peace with everyone. Do not take revenge, my friends, but leave room for God's wrath, for it is written: "It is mine to avenge; I will repay, says the Lord. On the contrary: "If your enemy is hungry, feed him; if he is thirsty, give him something to drink. In doing this, you will heap burning coals on his head. Do not be overcome by evil, but overcome evil with good.

There are special blessings for peace makers although it is not easy to be a peace maker. The advantages however, far exceed being a trouble maker. James 3:18 says 'Peacemakers who sow in peace raise a harvest of righteousness'.

4. Help weak people to overcome their weakness, and help others achieve their dreams

Do you know that nothing in nature is for itself? Rivers do not drink water; fruit bearing trees do not eat fruits. The sun does not use heat. Living for others is one of the best ways of living life. 'We who are strong ought to bear the fallings of the weak and not to please ourselves. Any person you come in contact with becomes your neighbour. Each one of us should please his neighbour for their good, to build them up. For even Christ did not please Himself but, as it is written: The insults of those who insult you have fallen on me' (Romans 15:1-3). Help the weak and vulnerable people as best as you can. Do not take advantage of them, or look down on them.

5. Deal with your own bad attitudes (James 3:2-3)

In order to build healthy and beneficial relationships, you must learn to deal with attitudes that do not promote togetherness. In other words, learn to change bad habits, start with yourself and examine the things you do that can offend the other person. James 3:2 says, we all stumble in many ways. If anyone is never at fault in what he says, he is a perfect man, able to keep his whole body in check'. None of us is perfect, and we have to apply that into all our dealings including our relationship with others. Jesus tells us in Matthew 7:3-5 this:

> Why do you look at the speck of sawdust in your brother's eye and pay no attention to the plank in your own eye? How can you say to your brother, Let me take the speck out of your eye, when all the time there is a plank in your own eye? You hypocrite, first take the plank out of your own eye, and then you will see clearly to remove the speck from your brother's eye.

In particular, why do you open your eyes to any fault of your brother, while you yourself are guilty of a much greater fault? Please learn to deal with your own attitudes, consistent change in character is a necessary requirement for any healthy and beneficial relationship.

6. Learn to settle disagreements

Disagreements and conflicts are inevitable in any relationship but we must learn to settle our differences amicably. Sadly, many people do not know how to settle problems in their relationships, and so they allow their problems to destroy their friendship.

The Bible, which is the word of God, offers many helpful ways to solve disagreement in relationships. Ephesians 4:26-27 says, 'In your anger do not sin, do not let the sun go down while you are still angry, do not give the devil a foothold'. This text is particularly useful, if you are in an angry mood. The advice here is that do not go to bed with anger in your heart, else the enemy may capitalize on it and magnify the problem by given you negative feelings towards the person who wronged you. Matthew 18:15-17 gives further direction:

> If your brother sins against you, go and show him his fault, just between the two of you. If he listens to you, you have won your brother over. But if he will not listen, take one or two others along, so that every matter may be established by the testimony of two or three witnesses. If he refuses to listen to them, tell it to the church; and if he refuses to listen even to the church, treat him as you would a pagan or a tax collector.

The text you just read tells what to do if someone wrongs you and both of you happens to be a member of a church. The same principles can be applied in every situation. When someone wrongs you, go and show the person their fault. If he or she listens to you, good, if not get two or three matured people, and go to the person. If he or she still does not listen, report the matter to the church leadership, or any recognised leadership. If the person does not listen still to the leadership, then you can treat that person as an unbeliever- meaning we have to witness to the person all over again as an unbeliever or we have to treat the person as someone who needs help. There may be times, when you may have to allow the person to leave your company, if that is what he or she wants. When the prodigal son wanted to leave the house, his father allowed him (Luke 15:11-32).

To err they say, is human! So what happens when you wrong someone? Many people do not know what to do when they realise that they have sinned against someone. Some people ignore it; others think it does not matter. Ignoring it can hinder your blessings and can harm the relationship or hurt the other party, or you can even be punished. Matthew 5:23-25 offers some helpful guidance:

> Therefore, if you are offering your gift at the altar and there remember that your brother has something against you; leave your gift there in front of the altar. First go and be reconciled to your brother; then come and offer your gift. Settle matters quickly with your adversary who is taking you to court. Do it while you are still with him on the way, or he may hand you over to the judge, and the judge may hand you over to the officer, and you may be thrown into prison.

If you wrong someone, please first go to the person you have offended, and ask for forgiveness and seek peace. In this way, the relationship can be restored. There is one thing which makes resolving conflict difficult and I would discuss this briefly in the next paragraph before we look at the next guideline.

One of the things which make resolving issues difficult is what I call 'the third unseen voice' coming from someone who advises one of the parties secretly. For example, when a man and his wife have a problem, and if there is someone else advising either the man or the woman on what to do or which direction to go without the knowledge of the other partner, the voice of this third person is what I call' the third unseen voice'. There can be no settlement of dispute unless this unseen voice is exposed or silenced. This voice can also come from an enemy speaking in one of the parties mind, or a voice speaking to the person in a dream or in a vision. As long as this voice is not silenced, there can be no settlement of disputes.

7. The Golden Rule- Treat people how you want them to treat you

In any kind of relationship, it advisable to treat the other partner the way you would expect him or her to treat you. If the man will treat his wife as queen, the woman will also treat the man as king. This can help address selfishness and abuse in any relationship. This is known as 'the golden rule' and has its semblance in almost all religions in the world. Jesus' version is far more open-ended and challenging:

> So in everything, do to others what you would have them do to you, for this sums up the Law and the Prophets (Matthew 7:12).

Husbands, treat your wives in the same way you will want to be treated if you were the wife. The same applies to the wife. This rule is applicable in every facet of life including employee-employer relationship; church leader and congregation relationship. This is one of the ways to build a healthy relationship.

8. Draw closer to God

In order to build a healthy relationship, it is advisable to draw closer to God, your creator so that you can draw the needed strength to love, because God is full of love (1 John 4:7). Draw closer to God for protection. Sometimes our loved ones can do things that can hurt us in a very bad way. We will need strength and protection from God if we are to continue in the relationship.

It is a fact of life that in any kind of relationship, it is possible that one of the parties can run out of love, what I call 'the spike' of the relationship at some point in time. But since God is love (1 John 4:8), those who will draw closer to him will renew their love for their partner; they will receive strength to love again. God's love is shared abroad in our heart (Romans, 5:5); in the same way his mercies are renewed every morning (Lamentation 3:22-23). As believers, we can also be rest assured that the source where we draw our capital from never runs dry. The book of Isaiah 40: 29-31 tells us that 'God gives strength to the weary and increases the power of the weak. Even youths grow tired and weary, and young men stumble and fall; but those who hope in the LORD will renew their strength'.

Jesus teaches us to pray to God not to lead us into temptation but deliver us from the evil one (Matthew 6:13). Draw closer to God so that He will guide you from temptations, and also keep you from harm. You can make the prayer of a man called Jabez your prayer too:

> Jabez was more honorable than his brothers. His mother had named him Jabez, saying, I gave birth to him in pain. Jabez cried out to the God of Israel, Oh, that you would bless me and enlarge my territory! Let your hand be with me, and keep me from harm so that I will be free from pain. And God granted his request (1 Chronicles 4:9-10).

The good God, who created the heavens and the earth, protect you, enlarge your territory and keep you free from harm as you read this book.

9. Have four circles of friends or four levels of association

In order to build healthy relationships, it is advisable to have levels or circles of association: Friends in the world, Christian friends, Close Christian friends, and the innermost friendship between you and God as shown in the diagram below.

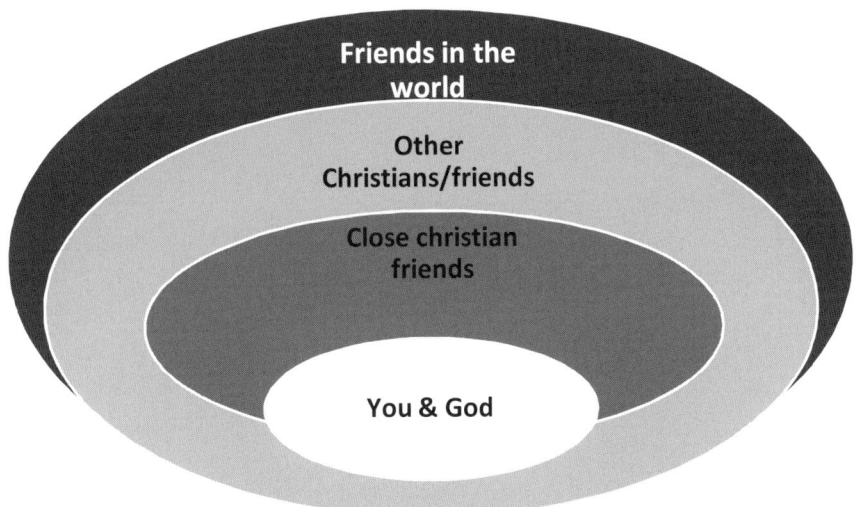

Diagram :1 Circles of friendship

This diagram is an illustration of how you can build levels of friendship. You should not allow just anybody at all to be in your inner circle, they may mess you up. Let us discuss these circles one after another.

A. Friends in the World

These type of friendship, are people who are outside your faith tradition. You can call them worldly friends. Do not expect too much from them, else you may be disappointed; but be a light to them.

B. Christian friends (if you are a Christian)

These are friends or people who share the same faith with you. These are your brothers and sisters in the Lord.

C. Close Christian friends

This circle of friendship is what I will describe as your either twelve or three disciples. I drew this inspiration from how Jesus selected three of His disciples from among the twelve (Matthew 26:36-37). In the same manner, get people who truly love you, who are willing to share your dreams, faith, and your life aspirations and bring them close to yourself, but with caution. These people should be your close friends; they can be three or twelve. But you need another level of relationship apart from these three close friends. Because even these close friends can desert you just as the Psalmist in the Bible experienced. He says 'Even my close friend, someone I trusted, one who shared my bread, has turned against me. But you, O LORD, have mercy on me; raise me up, that I may repay them' (Psalm 41:9-10). We complain, and justly so, of the want of sincerity, and it is true that there is scarcely any true friendship to be found among men. In this text, one particular friend, in whom the psalmist had reposed great confidence, took part with his enemies. Like how Judas betrayed Jesus to his enemies. But let us not think it strange, if we receive evil treatment from those who are supposed to be our friends. You can decide to allow the evil treatment to get at you, or shake it off and move on. The hurt we suffer when our friends betray us should teach us not to betray anyone. God is also hurt when we are not right with Him. How do you treat God?

D. The Innermost friendship- You and your Friendship with God

There comes a time when your only true companion will be God, who will never fail you. All your friends can desert you for various reasons. Either they will not have enough love or stamina to be by your side because of what you are going through, or maybe they may be fed up with you. Even Jesus had all his disciples abandoned Him at some point (Matthew 26: 31-35). His only hope was the relationship He had with the Father in heaven. You can also have this relationship with God; He is your Father too. A righteous man called Job experienced the same abandonment by his wife and friends when he lost all his property and his health (Job 1-2). But Job had hope in God. He said, 'But as for me, I know that my Redeemer lives, and he will stand upon the earth at last' (Job 19:25).

So far, we have been discussing the subject of social capital. We defined this capital as the strength, love, support and the encouragement we draw from our fellow humans to help us achieve our God given dreams in life. Human beings are spiritual, social, and material. Let us look at the last of our capitals to be discussed in this book.

5.5 Material Capital

Spiritual capital, social capital, and material capital; these three capitals are all essential for your survival, but in order of priority, the most important one, as we have already mentioned is the spiritual capital followed by social capital, and then the material capital. In this section we will be discussing what is material capital, how to obtain it and how to prioritise it so that it will not stand in the way of your salvation (spiritual capital).

What is material capital?

Simply speaking, material capital as the word suggests is anything material, not spiritual or social, and this can include funds and other goods, which can all be measured quite accurately by money. Others refer to it as financial capital. Material capital is mainly measured in monetary terms or material terms. Material capital is very important. Without it, you will cease to be a human being.

How to obtain decent material capital

The Bible says in Proverbs 10:4-5 that 'Lazy hands make a man poor, but diligent hands bring wealth. He who gathers crops in summer is a wise son, but he who sleeps during harvest is a disgraceful son. To acquire material capital, you must work hard, try to be fair, not robbing anyone, not engaging in any business that poses danger to other people. Hard work and diligence can secure your financial wealth, but we need to be careful that the pursuance of material capital does not consume us at the detriment of our salvation. The word of God gives us this advice: 'We should not wear ourselves out in our quest to get rich, but we must have the wisdom to show restraint' (Proverbs 23:4).

The rich young ruler Complex

We all cannot be rich, as the scripture says, 'there will never cease to be poor people in the land' (Deuteronomy, 15:11). In the same way, not all of us will be poor. The world will always produce both rich and poor people. But the tragedy is that most people will not repent of their sins and turn to follow Jesus for the salvation of their soul when they are at the top of the mountain. Most of us find God in the valleys of our lives not on the mountain tops. It is when we are confronted with our limitations, sickness or a tragedy, that we turn to God and confess our need of him. But this should not be so.

In Jesus' days on earth, one of the people who really desired to be saved yet walked away from Jesus was a rich young ruler. This rich man was impressed by Jesus and wanted to know how he could obtain eternal life. However, he rejected what Jesus told him because it meant he would have to 'sell all that he had, and distribute the proceeds to the poor, and then he would have treasures in heaven'. After giving all his wealth to the poor he is to follow Jesus Christ. The Bible says 'When he heard this, he became very sad, because he was a man of great wealth. Jesus looked at him and said, 'How hard it is for the rich to enter the kingdom of God' (Luke 18: 23-24).

Of course, it was not the riches in and of themselves that were evil, but Jesus knew that this particular rich man would choose riches over Him as the Lord of his life. Relatively, few wealthy people throughout history have truly followed Jesus. This is one of the reasons why North America and Western Europe are not experiencing massive conversion of souls compared to other parts of the world. In Western Europe, people hardly go to church compared to people in other parts of the world. Sadly, many people in places where God is less worshipped are not content in life. There is a spiritual hunger in the life of these people, but they do not know where to turn to be fed spiritually because most of them do not see God and His church as the true source of spiritual help. Material capital is good only if we do not allow it to blind us to spiritual things.

In rich societies, even most of the few men and women, who respond to the gospel, do it with less enthusiasm and seriousness. Jesus Christ describes people who receive Him with less enthusiasm and seriousness because of their riches as follows:

> You say I am rich; I have acquired wealth and do not need a thing. But you do not realize that you are wretched, pitiful, poor, blind and naked. I counsel you to buy from me gold refined in the fire, so you can become rich; and white clothes to wear, so you can cover your shameful nakedness; and salve to put on your eyes, so you can see(Revelation 3:17-18).

There is a great danger in self-deception. These people in fact did not know their real spiritual state. They thought they were rich, either materially or spiritually but they were wrong and so Jesus declared them unqualified to enter the kingdom of God. They were rich in worldly goods but their very wealth led them to a quiet aggressive kind of religion. They were proud, also of their intellectual wealth; self- complacent in comfortable worldly circumstances, and became puffed up with a vain philosophy, they learned to be satisfied with their spiritual state, and to believe the best of themselves, and then to believe in themselves. They are hypocrites, who did not know they were hypocrites. They thought themselves to be good; and this self-deception was their danger. To use Prof. Mozley's words:

> Why should a man repent of his goodness? He may well repent, indeed, of his falsehood; but unhappily the falsehood of it is just the thing he does not see, and which he cannot see by the very law of his character. Who is to convert the hypocrite? A hypocrite person does not know he is a hypocrite; he cannot upon the very basis of his character; he sees himself as a sincere person; and the more he is in the shackles of his own character, i.e., the greater hypocrite he is, the more sincere he thinks of himself.

Material capital is needed for survival by everybody. What is needed is a balanced priority, where we place the need for spiritual capital above all other capitals.

5.6 The unfortunate rejection of God as the source of all capital and its demise

The rejection of God as the source of all capitals by some people, especially in Western countries, has rendered many people in these societies the inability to cope with life tragedies. When people are in trouble they do not look to God for help because they have not been taught how to seek the Lord. Help from God is free! Unfortunately, many people reject God, and act in ways that undermines his sovereignty over them. This rejection can be in three different ways. The first is the denial of the doctrine of depravity and the need for God's grace. The second is through ungratefulness for what God has done. The third is the total denial of the existence of God. Let us discuss this ways of rejection one by one.

1. The Denial of the doctrine of depravity and the Need for God's Grace

In the West, and especially in the United States, a form of 'cultural Pelagianism' seems to be gaining ground. Pelagianism was a movement based in Rome in the early fifth century that asserted that human beings were in total control of their situation. This movement started with a man called Pelagius who denied the doctrine of depravity and the need for God's grace. The doctrine of depravity teaches that: Mankind's heart is evil (Mark 7:21-23), and sick (Jeremiah 17:9). Mankind is a slave of sin (Romans 7:15-25). Mankind does not seek God unless told to do so (Romans 3:10-12). Mankind cannot understand spiritual things (1 Corinthians 2:14). Mankind is at enmity with God (Ephesians 2:15) and by nature deserves the wrath of God because we do not do what is right (Ephesians. 2:3).

It is a fact of life that everyone has weaknesses, and limitations. God, who made us, describes this human condition as a 'sinful condition'. The apostle Paul writes: 'For all have sinned, and come short of the glory of God' (Romans 3:23). Let us note in general terms the large truths which this passage contains. Everyone falls short of, miss their own expectation, or fail to obtain the glory of God or fall short of God's expectation. If this is the case, where then can human beings turn to for help? How can we overcome this sinful attitude, and who can cure our heart of this wickedness? We need a higher being, more superior than any human being.

This higher being is God, the creator of the universe (Acts 17:24). John Piper, in his article *Towards a Deeper Experience of God's Grace* defines God's grace as *the heart of God to do you good when you deserve it least*. I define God's grace as God's unmerited favour towards humanity. God's grace is when He decides to help someone to be born again, to receive healing, to give a barren person a child, or even to change someone's destiny for good when the individual has not really worked to earn such goodness. Many people have received grace from God to help them change their lives. Paul of Tarsus has the following to say about the subject of God's grace:

> I thank Christ Jesus our Lord, who has given me strength, that he considered me faithful, appointing me to his service. Even though I was once a blasphemer and a persecutor and a violent man, I was shown mercy because I acted in ignorance and unbelief. The grace of our Lord was poured out on me abundantly, along with the faith and love that are in Christ Jesus (1 Timothy 1:12-14).

Paul persecuted the church of God initially because he thought the early Christians were blasphemous of the Jewish laws. He was an ardent promoter of the persecutions of Christians until he had an encounter with Jesus. That encounter changed his view about Christianity and his personal life. This is what the grace of God can do, changing a persecutor of believers to become a promoter of the kingdom message. The grace of God can help you to stop even your most undesired attitudes such as drinking, smoking, womanizing, stealing, and to have control of your anger. It is this same grace that changed my life to become a servant of God. I am glad I received the Lord into my life when the opportunity came.

The grace of God comes to people in different ways depending on their unique situation. Those who are sick receive grace for healing, those who are spiritually lost, heading to hell receive the grace to be born again, and those who are weak and powerless receive the grace to be strong. But the Lord said to me, 'My grace is sufficient for you, for my power is made perfect in weakness. Therefore I will boast all the more gladly about my weaknesses, so that Christ's power may rest on me' (2 Corinthians 12:9). It is rather unfortunate for people to reject God as the true source of all that we need. It is even tragic when people do not go to God for help in times of crisis. It is my prayer that as you read this book, you will open your heart, for the Lord to bestow His grace upon you in a special way.

The incarnation of Jesus Christ as discussed earlier on, is one of the ways God chose to help the human race in our sinful condition. The Incarnation is a fundamental theological teaching of Christianity. The doctrine of incarnation is the belief that the Son of God, who is the non-created second *hypostasis* of the triune God, took on a human body and nature and became both man and God (in essence or nature). In the Bible, its clearest teaching is in John 1:14: 'And the Word became flesh, and dwelt among us'.

The angels fell, and remained without hope or help. Christ never designed to be the Saviour of the fallen angels, therefore He did not take their nature; and the nature of angels could not be an atoning sacrifice for the sin of mankind. Here is a price paid, enough for all, and suitable to all, for it was in our nature. Here, the wonderful love of God appeared, that when Christ knew what He must suffer, and how He must die in it, yet he readily took it upon Himself. And this atonement made way for people's deliverance from Satan's bondage, and for the pardon of their sins through faith. Let those who dread death, and strive to get the better of their terrors, no longer attempt to outbrave or to stifle them, no longer grow careless or wicked through despair. Let them not expect help from the world, or human devices alone; but let them seek pardon, peace, grace, and a lively hope of heaven, by faith in Him who died and rose again, that thus they may rise above the fear of death.

Unfortunately, this denial of the doctrine of depravity and the rejection of God's grace has become the way a lot of people in Western societies in particular live. This culture is passed on from one generation to the next. They deny the fact that they are sinners, and that they need the grace of God. They are confident in themselves and their human achievements. This over confidence worldview overlooked the tragic side of human depravity with its obvious weakness and failings. Because of this, many people in the West are not able to cope with pressures of life. Many easily get stressed and depressed over little issues. But this seems not to be the case for people in societies that have accepted their weaknesses and limitations and are seeking help from heaven.

Societies or people who have acknowledged God in their lives receive help from heaven when they are in need. The prophet Isaiah says, *those who hope in the Lord will renew their strength* (Isaiah 40: 31).

Just as Pelagius declared that human beings have total control over themselves and their destinies, modern Western societies want to believe that it can control every aspect of life. In spite of the technological advancement, Western societies might have accepted that it cannot defeat death; neither can they control human suffering. Pelagianism was at heart a delusion, but a delusion that many people passionately wanted to believe. They did not want to face up to the hard facts of life, which suggested that human beings were not in total control of things and needed the grace of God if they were to survive and to endure lasting prosperity, body, spirit, and soul.

As a result of rejecting the doctrine of depravity and the need for God's grace, many people do not know the Spiritual and God's Kingdom recourses for coping with life challenges. There are a lot of help in God's kingdom to cope with life challenges. Secondly, many have turned to unhelpful places for solutions to their problems instead of turning to God- they are fitting square pegs in round holes. Those of us in the West seem to spend a lot of our resources on solving problems than learning to live well. Many people wait till their marriages or relationships hit the rock before seeking help from professional counsellors. Many parents in developed countries wait till their teenagers are imprisoned before they start looking for mentors for them instead of training the children the way of the Lord.

Suffering, which is one of the tragedies of life, does not seem to have been a major philosophical problem in the Middle Ages, neither is it today for countless millions in Africa and Latin America. This is because these societies have the cultural, spiritual and human resources to cope with sufferings because God is at the centre of their lives. But in our highly developed societies of the West, suffering is a philosophical problem, perhaps because our societies have long lost sight of the cultural and spiritual resources for coping with it. They simply lack the spiritual capital.

It is not my aim to discuss the subject of human suffering in its entirety in this book. I am discussing it here to illustrate the truth that human beings need help from God since we have not been able to solve the problem of human suffering. For those of us who want to read further about human suffering, Dr. R.C. Sproul has written an excellent book on the subject of suffering which you will find very helpful. The title is: *SURPIRISED BY SUFFERING: THE ROLE OF PAIN AND DEATH IN THE CHRISTIAN LIFE.*

Suffering is a painful reminder of the limitations of the human nature and human culture. Suffering hurts because its point to definite and disconcerting limits to human abilities. This explains the paradox that Westerners, who are among the most privileged of human race, who enjoy standards of living that are astonishing by other standards and who through excellent medical services, suffer less than anyone else make suffering into a big theological and philosophical problem than it need be. Westerners see third world countries as economic sufferers. But people in poor countries do not always see themselves that way. In fact, it seems people in third world countries who have God at the centre of their lives are more content in life than most people in developed societies who do not make God the centre of their lives.

So what is the way forward? I think we need to recover our awareness of our limitations as human beings, and to seek divine help from God. Despite all human advances in civilization, we have never been able to give an answer to the problem of suffering. We need to accept our limitations and realize that, on account of them, suffering will be an inevitable part of human existence. We therefore need help from God.

God wants to give us all the capitals. But this is a choice people must make on their own accord. Unfortunately, many people are only concerned with material capital, and so become malnourished spiritually and socially. Many rich people are not content because they lack the spiritual and social capitals. On the basis of global survey of religious values, wealth and well being do not necessarily equate with spiritual satisfaction. It may also be said that, despite wealth and political stability, people in western societies do not always feel secure. In 'secure' societies, people's overall sense of wellbeing ceases to increase with per capita income but people may continue to try to improve their lives by developing a spiritual dimension. This is one of the reasons why there is a continued prevalence of spiritual values and religious concerns in Western society.

Research upon research has shown that church attendance is in decline in Western countries. But what may be happening in the West is that, people are changing the way in which they exercise faith, and one way of expressing this is a shift from religion to spirituality. Whereas religion is practiced through membership of a congregation, spirituality is an individual pursuit only loosely associated with others. But these changes in the spiritual landscape in the west can be very dangerous for a number of reasons. I have discussed some of these reasons in my book, *Building your Life on the Principles of God: The Solid foundation*.

Let us discuss the second way people unfortunately turn back on God as the source of their capitals.

2. Turning back on God after a blessing

The second way people reject God as the source of their capital is the turning back on God after the Lord has blessed them. In time of crisis, many people turn to God for help but once they are helped by the Lord they turn their backs on God and live anyhow. They stop going to the house of God to worship him. They stop making contributions to the growth of their church. I am aware that some of these people are ignorant; such people need to be taught the word of God. A typical example in the Bible is the account between Jesus and the ten lepers who were miraculous healed by Jesus Christ:

> Now on his way to Jerusalem, Jesus traveled along the border between Samaria and Galilee. As He was going into a village, ten men who had leprosy met him. They stood at a distance and called out in a loud voice, Jesus, Master, have pity on us! When he saw them, he said, Go, and show yourselves to the priests. And as they went, they were cleansed. One of them, when he saw he was healed, came back, praising God in a loud voice. He threw himself at Jesus' feet and thanked him—and he was a Samaritan. Jesus asked, were not all ten cleansed? Where are the other nine? Was no one found to return and give praise to God except this foreigner? Then he said to him, Rise and go; your faith has made you well (Luke 17:11-18).

When we thank God for His blessings, He blesses us more. Even as you read this book, my prayer for you is that the grace of God that is reaching more and more people over the whole world should locate you, and help you overcome any challenge you face in Jesus name. But please, do not be like any of the nine lepers who after receiving their healing never went back to thank Jesus. Thanksgiving is an act of worship to God, especially if it is done in the name of the Lord. Among the ten lepers who got healed, only one of them came back to thank Jesus and so Jesus declared further blessings upon him,' Rise and go; your faith has made you well'.

The whole ten set off at once. They had got all they wanted from the Lord, and had no more thought about Him. So they turned their backs on Him. How strange it must have been to feel, as they went along, the gradual creeping of soundness into their bones! How much more confidently they may have stepped out, as the glow of returning health asserted itself more and more! The cure is a transcendent, though veiled, manifestation of Christ's power; for it is wrought at a distance, without even a word, and with no vehicle. It is simply the silent forth-putting of His power. 'He spoke, and it was done'.

The nine might have said, 'We are doing what the Healer bade us do; to go back to Him would be disobedience.' But a grateful heart knows that to express gratitude is the highest form of obedience. How like us all it is to hurry away clutching our blessings, and never cast back a thought to the giver! This leper's voice had returned to Him, and his 'loud' acknowledgments were very different from the strained croak of his petition for healing. He knew that he had to thank God and Jesus; he did not know that these two were one. His healing has brought him much nearer to Jesus than before, and now he can fall at His feet. Thankfulness knits us to Jesus with a blessed bond. Nothing is as sweet to a loving heart as to pour itself out in thanks to Him.

There are many lessons we can learn from this incident and there are many ways people turn their back on God after they have received blessings. For example, when you have prayed to God for something, and refused to worship Him regularly in His church after you have received answer to your prayer. When you marry in the church and stop going to church afterwards can be considered as another way of turning your back on God. When you are baptised in the church but stop going to church is also not good. You will not be made whole. When you present your child to the Lord in dedication in the church and stop attending church service regularly with the child, it is also another way of turning your back on God. Some people too are very smart, they will go to a particular church for a specific need, and after they have received their breakthrough in that church, they will leave and join another church. These are all unfaithful practices, an act of disloyalty.

But why would people turn their back on God after receiving blessings? There are many reasons. Some people do not know that they have to continue to make the worship of God a priority. Such people may see God as an 'old man' who is just there to provide our needs. It is true that God is our Father in heaven and our provider, but He is also calling us into a Father-child relationship, where He expects us to make His worship the number one priority of our lives. What this means in practical terms is that we must pray to Him regularly, worship him in the church, love one another, stay away from sin and unholy life, help build His kingdom on earth by winning souls and also by given our material resources to sponsor mission projects. It is the duty of the church to keep on teaching people these principles. The people have the duty to humbly accept the word of God as they are being taught.

> Because of the LORD'S great love we are not consumed, for His compassions never fail. They are new every morning; great is your faithfulness (Lamentations 3:22-23).

We are alive today because of the love and mercies of God. We slept last night and He watched over us till the morning when we woke up. Even the air we breathe is enough for us to give thanks to God. If God were to deny us that for a moment we will not be able to survive. Do you know how God has been protecting you from Satan and evil people? The Bible warns us: 'Be self-controlled and alert. Your enemy the devil prowls around like a roaring lion looking for someone to devour' (1 Peter 5:8).

The truth is that we do not deserve what God gives us. For example, if God has to place you on a scale and weigh your good deeds and thoughts against your bad deeds and thoughts, what will be your position? But God does not treat us this way. In fact He gives us numerous chances and resources to change and better our lives. Regarding our salvation, the Bible says 'God demonstrates His own love for us in this: While we were still sinners, Christ died for us. Since we have now been justified by his blood, how much more shall we be saved from God's wrath through Him (Romans 5:8-9).

In this section we have been looking at the second way people unfortunately turn back on God as the source of their capital: they turn back on God after God has blessed them. Let us look at the last of these three ways people reject God as the provider of their capitals in the next section.

3. Total denial of the existence of God and its demise

When Yuri Gagarin returned to the USSR from his space flight, and reported that he has not seen God, a Russian Orthodox priest remarked 'if you haven't seen him on earth, you will never see him in heaven'. When people say there is no God, what they mean in essence is that there is no God in their lives. Believe me, there is God that rule in the affairs of men in this world. Just examine the life of people, who says there is no God, you will find out that indeed there is no God in their lives. Someone once said, 'A life without Christ is full of Crisis'. To deny the existence of God is to set the stage for being cut off from eternal life, and any other kingdom blessings that come with it. The implication of such stance is that people won't go for the many blessings God is willing to give His creation.

God exist! He is the creator of the universe. He owns the whole world and everything in it including every human beings and Satan himself. Jesus talked about God the Father and urged the people to believe in Him (John 14:1). He did not argue for or against the existence of God. The Christian community should continue to help people to believe in God by sharing the gospel of Jesus Christ with them; they should help people overcome their unbelief (Mark 9:24). There are many reasons why people deny the existence of God or do not believe in God. Some people have not been introduced to this God who created the heavens and the earth. Some people too do not want to believe in God, because believing in God demands a change of lifestyle from bad to good. But some of these people are not ready to change. It is important to note that whatever their stance is, it does not exempt them from being accountable to God on the judgement day.

In this chapter, we have been looking at how we can prioritise our spiritual capital, social capital, and materials. The next chapter will look at some examples of balanced priorities.

Chapter 6

Some examples of balanced priorities

My hope is that, by now you have convinced yourself of the importance of prioritising your life. In this chapter, we will look at some examples of balanced priorities. You can apply the principles discussed in this section to your own life.

6.1 The need to prioritize when something is entrusted to you

Life is a gift from God in much the same way as the salvation of the human soul. The parable of the sower in Luke 8:1-15 tells us that only twenty five percent of people who received divine blessings became fruitful. The rest lost all that they received. One way to guard these life treasures is to learn to set your priorities right once you receive them. Sometimes, it may mean that you have to learn to pray more or change the circles of your friends or even acquire new skills or even seek further understanding.

> Timothy, guard what has been entrusted to your care. Turn away from godless chatter and the opposing ideas of what is falsely called knowledge, which some have professed and in so doing have wandered from the faith (1 Timothy 6:20).

> Now it is required that those who have been given a trust must prove faithful (1 Corinthians 4:2).

In this challenging world, count it a blessing if you have someone to help you set your priorities right. In the text read, a young man called Timothy was told to turn away from godless chatter and to be faithful with what has been entrusted into his care. When something precious is entrusted into your care, you may be required to reset your priorities in order to live up to the demands of the new opportunity.

Many people have lost precious things that came their way because they were unable to guard them. 2 John 1:8 says 'Watch out that you do not lose what you have worked for, but that you may be rewarded fully'. You must also bear in mind that whatever God gives you is for the benefit of the larger society. Many destinies are connected to your success. If you do well in life, many people will be blessed as well. Many people are suffering in this world because their predecessors failed to pass on blessings to them. So please take good care of what you have and make sure you can pass it on to others.

Some of the things that can be entrusted into one's care include the following; businesses, a vision, leadership role, an inheritance, a particular talent, ministry, and spiritual gifts. All these 'treasures' are for the common good of all people and so it is important that you take very good care of them.

Sometimes, you may have to improve your personal security so that you will not lose them to 'predators'. If you are a born again Christian, the Holy Spirit can help you to guard anything that will be entrusted into your care:

> Guard the good deposit that was entrusted to you--guard it with the help of the Holy Spirit who lives in us (2 Timothy 1:14).

The Holy Spirit gives wisdom from heaven. He counsels, He directs believers to all truth and the best way to live their lives (John 14:16; 16:13). There are two main types of wisdom: earthly wisdom and Godly wisdom which comes from above. The wisdom that comes from heaven is first of all pure; then peace-loving, considerate, submissive, full of mercy and good fruit, impartial and sincere (James 3:17). You can get this wisdom by simply asking God for it in prayer.

When Joshua took over the leadership from Moses in leading the Israelites to the promised, one of the things God told him was for him to be strong and courageous. Joshua was told to build a strong and courageous character because of the new assignment:

> Be strong and very courageous. Be careful to obey all the law my servant Moses gave you; do not turn from it to the right or to the left, that you may be successful wherever you go (Joshua 1:7).

A new spirit, a new leader! New seasons calls for new way of doing things. Joshua needed courage and to be strong. As a wife or husband what sort of character do you need? Maybe more love, more patience, and more goodness? Renewing your mind is part of character formation! When the church at Rome received the gospel of Jesus Christ, the apostle Paul wrote to them the need for them to renew their mind as follows:

> Do not conform any longer to the pattern of this world, but be transformed by the renewing of your mind. Then you will be able to test and approve what God's will is—his good, pleasing and perfect will (Roams 12:2).

It is only by the renewal of their mind that they will be transformed in order to taste the goodness of God.

Similarly, the apostle Peter wrote to the church reminding them of the need to add certain spiritual qualities to their new faith in order to make their calling and election sure. The quotation is somehow lengthy but it is full of insights, read on:

> His divine power has given us everything we need for life and godliness through our knowledge of Him who called us by His own glory and goodness. Through these He has given us His very great and precious promises, so that through them you may participate in the divine nature and escape the corruption in the world caused by evil desires. For this very reason, make every effort to add to your faith goodness; and to goodness, knowledge; and to knowledge, self-control; and to self-control, perseverance; and to perseverance, godliness; and to godliness, brotherly kindness; and to brotherly kindness, love. For if, you possess these qualities in increasing measure, they will keep you from being ineffective and unproductive in your knowledge of our Lord Jesus Christ. But if anyone does not have them, he is nearsighted and blind, and has forgotten that he has been cleansed from his past sins. Therefore, my brothers, be all the more eager to make your calling and election sure. For if you do these things, you will never fall, and you will receive a rich welcome into the eternal kingdom of our Lord and Savior Jesus Christ (2 Peter 1:3-11).

The writer says add these qualities to your faith, in increasing measure. This will make you effective, you will never fall, and you will receive a rich welcome into the eternal kingdom of God. Improve upon your character by adding those virtues you think you lack. If you lack self-control, find ways and means to be self-controlled. If you lack godliness, train yourself to be godly. If you are not well acquitted with the teachings about the kingdom of God, get this knowledge. You can apply this principle of adding virtues to the blessings you have received in every area of your life. For example, a married man will have to add certain virtues to his marriage. The same applies to a woman; else it's likely the marriage will suffer unnecessarily.

Let us talk about the need to prioritize your friends or the people around you. Sometimes, it may be necessary to prioritize or manage the type of people you move with when something precious is entrusted into your care. Psalm 1 offers a helpful advice:

> Blessed is the man who does not walk in the counsel of the wicked or stand in the way of sinners or sit in the seat of mockers. But his delight is in the law of the LORD, and on His law he meditates day and night. He is like a tree planted by streams of water, which yields its fruit in season and whose leaf does not wither. Whatever he does prospers (Psalm 1:1-3).

Some friends are very good and helpful. Others too, are aimless and trouble makers. If you allow trouble makers or aimless people to stay close to you, they may destroy what has been entrusted into your care. So watch out! Blessed is the man who does not walk in the counsel of the wicked nor stand in the way of sinners nor sit in the seat of mockers. Mockers are people who laugh at other people's effort, and discourage them. They themselves have nothing to do or they may have neglected their post or duty. Get the right people around you.

During the days of Abraham, the father of faith, do you know that when Ishmael mocked Isaac, God allowed Ishmael to be sent away from his father's house?

> The child grew and was weaned, and on the day Isaac was weaned Abraham held a great feast. But Sarah saw that the son [Ishmael] whom Hagar the Egyptian had borne to Abraham was mocking and she said to Abraham, "Get rid of that slave woman and her son, for that slave woman's son will never share in the inheritance with my son Isaac.

God himself does not like mockers. God told Abraham to listen to his wife Sarah's advice and send Ishmael and his mother Hagar away.

In Genesis chapter 12, God called Abraham and promised to bless him, so that through him the whole world will be blessed with the light of salvation. This promise by God to bless the whole world was fulfilled with the coming of Jesus Christ into the world to save sinners. Galatians 3:14 says 'He redeemed us in order that the blessing given to Abraham might come to the Gentiles through Christ Jesus, so that by faith we might receive the promise of the Spirit'. Whoever believes in Jesus Christ receives salvation of the soul and eternal life.

Isaac was chosen to inherit his father, Abraham regarding this great promise. Although every human being is special in the sight of God, this unique role made Isaac a special person to God and the world. People who have been entrusted with something precious should see themselves as very important to the lives of many people because they carry the destinies of many people. This is not to suggest that they should boast or see themselves better and others inferior; rather they should see themselves as servants, vessels chosen by God to be a blessing to many people.

Carefully choosing the type of friends you talk to and hang out with can also be another helpful way to guard what has been entrusted into your care. Some friends are like vultures. Others are 'heralds' who can help you achieve your dreams. Jesus said 'Wherever there is a carcass, there the vultures will gather' (Matthew 24:28). The vulture is a large, carnivorous bird that is most well-known for its scavenging nature. Friends who are like the vulture will come close to you to consume, and sometimes to destroy what has been entrusted into your care. Watch out! In order to walk with the right people, Sometimes God will permit the bad people in your life to hurt you so that you will detest their company. This is one of the ways God uses to separate faithful children from bad friends. Sometimes losing some friends is good! Someone once said, 'I asked God to protect me from my enemies, then I started losing friends'. Sometimes we lose friends the moment we start praying to God to protect us from evil and bad people; those we lose may not be good for us!

On the other hand, a herald 'is one who actively promotes or advocates' something. I pray that God sends a herald into your life to help you accomplish your purpose on earth. This is what God said to the prophet Habakkuk concerning a vision he received:

> Then the LORD replied: Write down the revelation and make it plain on tablets so that a herald may run with it (Habakkuk 2:2).

When a prophet is commanded in this manner, we can straight away tell the importance of such revelation. If you are a leader or a vision carrier, look for people who can support, run, and promote the vision and work with them. They are the ones you should spend more time and resources with. Explain the vision to them in the manner that they can understand. St. Paul advised Timothy his spiritual son as follows: 'And the things you have heard me say in the presence of many witnesses entrust to reliable men who will also be qualified to teach others (2 Timothy 2:2).

Timothy has been entrusted with something precious- the gospel of Jesus Christ, but he is to commit it to faithful men.—not to men who were merely 'believers' in Jesus Christ. This, of course, was intended, but the 'faithful men' here denoted loyal, trusty souls—men who, under no temptation, would betray the charge committed to them. Not only must the Christian leaders to whom Timothy is to give the commission of teaching, be trustworthy men, they must also possess knowledge and the power of communicating the knowledge to others. Look for reliable people and surround yourself with them. But make sure you yourself you are reliable too, and do not forget to build a strong personal relationship with God as well. You must also walk with people who are wise:

> He who walks with the wise grows wise, but a companion of fools suffers harm (Proverbs 13:20).

Walk with wise people and you can become wise. Walk with righteous people and you can become righteous because they may teach you the way of righteousness. But if you walk with fools, you may suffer harm. Do not even walk with the so called good people who do not support your vision. The book of Proverbs judges every thought or action by one standard: 'Is this wise?' The word *wisdom* brings up pictures of gray-haired old men muttering obscure philosophic maxims. But that is almost the opposite of what Proverbs means by the word. Wisdom is above all practical and down to earth. Young people as well as the old should exercise wisdom. Wisdom teaches us how to live base on the knowledge we have received. Wisdom combines understanding with discipline—the kind of discipline an athlete needs in training. It also adds a healthy dose of good common sense.

'By wisdom a house is built, and through understanding it is established' (Proverbs 24:3). How do you become a wise person? You must first begin to listen. Wisdom is freely available to those who will stop the mere talk, and start acting, paying attention to God and his Word. Listen to your godly parents who have something to offer, and to wise counselors. Anybody can become wise, Proverbs says. Wisdom is not reserved for brainy elite, but becoming wise requires self-discipline. To study and humbly seek wisdom at every opportunity, talking to and walking with the right people requires wisdom. I pray the Lord gives you a good dose of it as you seek his face.

6.2 The need to prioritise family life, career, and your spirituality

Family life, career, and your spiritual life are all important. But you need the right balance. This is what this section is about. Someone once said: 'Earlier, my priority was only work. I worked like a dog before I got married'.

After marriage, once you have a baby, time management is difficult. Your responsibilities change, your priorities change. And you have to concentrate on them if you have to work out your life. Your career is just a part of your life. Like the person I just quoted, once you have a family, there is the need to make a balance of your priorities; else you may put your family or job at risk. If you are a workaholic, please have time for your partner and children. It pays more to do so. Many women do not make time for their husbands and vice versa:

> Frankly, too many women treat their husbands as accessories instead of priorities. Laura Schlessinger.

We can rephrase the above quote as: 'too many men and women treat their partners as accessories instead of priorities'. Some men also, spend their quality time with other women outside their matrimonial home to the extent that by the time they get home they are too tired to spend romantic time with their wives. Some women too, become too busy with household chores to the extent that by the time they get to bed, they are too tired to have sex with their husbands. They have used all their energy in the kitchen, and the tiding up of the house. A woman may push her man to seek sexual satisfaction outside the marriage if she keeps on neglecting quality and healthy sexual lifestyle with the man and vice versa.

Inappropriate emotional intimacy: A married person must be very cautious about having a friend of the opposite sex. Ideally, your spouse should be your best friend. Pouring out your heart and sharing your emotions and feelings with someone of the opposite sex other than your spouse is emotional unfaithfulness. It displaces your spouse from her rightful position in your life. It creates an emotional distance between you and your spouse. And this can lead to marriage breakdown where you begin to feel like you do not love your partner anymore. Do not give too much emotional attention to other people other than your partner. Your spouse does not have to compete for your emotional attention with anyone. Most sexual encounters outside marriage are preceded by casual innocent friendships and inappropriate emotional intimacy. Safeguard your marriage;

honour and respect your spouse by cutting all inappropriate friendships and intimate ties with people of the opposite sex.

Another area that needs mentioning is married couples' relationship with God. Some people used to have good relationship with God, attend church service regularly, participate in most church activities, and live good Christian life. But once they get married, they begin to give excuses. Some even stop attending church service altogether once they get married. God gives us partners, so that our lives may be complete. It is therefore an act of ungratefulness for believers to use the gift of marriage and child bearing as an excuse for not worshipping God. Remember, the God we serve is a jealous God (Exodus, 20:5). It is possible that God is angry with those men and women who abandon worship once they get married. Priority is essential here.

When you were single, your priorities were different. Now that you are married with or without kids, there is the need to change or shift your priorities. Give most appropriate time to your family, yourself, your career, and ultimately your God.

6.3 Experiencing a miracle and living the Christian life

What is a miracle? A miracle is an extraordinary and welcome event believed to be the work of God. It suggests supernatural interference with nature or the course of events especially at a time when we cannot do much to help ourselves.

Why should God do miracles? First, God does miracles to meet our needs; both believers and unbelievers (Matthew 15:29-39). Sometimes, we can be discouraged by the plight of life- but Jesus brings us the Good News invitation; 'Come to me, all you who are weary and burdened, and I will give you rest' (Matthew 11:28). The second reason God does miracles in our lives is because, Satan who is the god of this age has blinded the minds of many people, so that they cannot see the light of the gospel of the glory of Christ, who is the image of God' (2 Corinthians 4:4). And so, God shines His light in our hearts to give us the light of the knowledge of the glory of God in the face of Christ' so that we can be saved or so that we can have spiritual understanding (2 Corinthians 4:6).

Sometimes, God has to step in to deliver people from darkness to light, like what Paul experienced on his way to Damascus as recorded in the book of Acts chapter 9. Salvation of the human soul is a miracle. No one can go to Jesus Christ for salvation unless God the Father draws that person to Jesus for salvation (John 6:44). The fourth reason why God does miracles is because *we are sometimes oppressed by demonic kingdoms from the devil and evil men.* The Bible tells as this: Put on the full armor of God so that you can take your stand against the devil's schemes. Our struggle is not against flesh and blood, but against the rulers, against the authorities, against the powers of this dark world and against the spiritual forces of evil in the heavenly realms (Ephesians 6:11-12).

Miracles themselves are tokens of God's kindness to us, because we are His creation, His handiwork. But it is not enough for us to receive miracles from God. God expects us to repent of our ways and to live in a relationship with Him; making the worship of His divinity a priority, and to love our fellow human beings. The book of Romans 2:4 says, 'or do you show contempt for the riches of His kindness, tolerance and patience, not realizing that God's kindness leads you towards repentance? If God has been kind to you, let His kindness encourage you to be more committed to Him and to His kingdom. This is what Jesus said to a man He healed at the temple: 'See, you are well again. Stop sinning or something worse may happen to you' (John 5:14).

Although miracles are good, they are not enough. What is required after experiencing a miracle is repentance and commitment to God and His kingdom. Surprisingly, seeing supernatural miracles did not lead many people to repent and to follow Jesus' teaching. Jesus was not happy with people who received miracles from Him yet did not repent:

> Then Jesus began to denounce the cities in which most of His miracles had been performed, because they did not repent. Woe to you, Korazin! Woe to you, Bethsaida! If the miracles that were performed in you had been performed in Tyre and Sidon, they would have repented long ago in

> sackcloth and ashes. But I tell you, it will be more bearable for Tyre and Sidon on the Day of Judgment than for you.
>
> And you, Capernaum, will you be lifted up to the skies? No, you will go down to the depths. If the miracles that were performed in you had been performed in Sodom, it would have remained to this day. But I tell you that it will be more

Throughout His ministry, Jesus showed annoyance with crowds who flocked to see a popular leader doing something supernatural. He wanted from them not applause, but commitment. Gradually, He relied more and more on parables, which, in private, He would explain to his disciples (Matthew 13:11-17). So if people want more from Jesus, then they must see Him in private.

There is the need for people to shift their attention or focus from miracles and begin to live the Christian life. Many church members are only looking forward to miracles instead of practically obeying the teachings of Jesus Christ and making the Great Commission a priority (Matthew 28:16-20). The church has a divine assignment to perform in this world. Our job is to go to all nations, and share the Good News: 'whoever believes and is baptized will be saved', to which every true believer is automatically called upon to be part of it. Let us discuss this subject further in the next section.

6.4 Balancing ministry and family life

Our aim in this section is to discuss how believers can balance ministry and family life. The reason for treating this subject is that some believers have abandoned the call of God upon their lives because of their marriage or children. Others too have only focused on the ministry and have neglected their family. We need a balance here. Let us look at the scriptural position concerning the first case:

> Anyone who loves his father or mother more than me is not worthy of me; anyone who loves his son or daughter more than me is not worthy of me (Matthew 10:37).

Where two affections come into collision, the weaker must give way; and though the man may not and ought not to cease to love, yet he must act as if he hated—disobey, and, it may be, desert—those to whom he is bound by natural ties, that he may obey the higher supernatural calling. The love of the family on no account takes precedence over love for Christ, but quite the reverse! The order of priority is to love God first, before all other things. Seek God's kingdom first and all other thing shall be added to you (Luke 12: 22-32). But let us discuss this subject further.

On the other hand, it is common to see some ministers neglecting their family responsibilities and focusing only on the church. This is especially true for ministers who travel a lot because of the great demand upon their ministry. No matter how busy one may be in ministry, it is required of them to take good care of their families:

> If anyone does not know how to manage his own family,
> how can he take care of God's church? (1 Timothy 3:5).

A well-ordered household, a decent behaviour, and the ability to demonstrate compassion to others, in my view are the test of a man's fitness or a woman's fitness to hold a high office in the public, and community of believers. As Theodoret observes, 'if a man cannot rule decorously a small community (such as a family), how shall he be judged a fit person to be entrusted with administration in a broader sphere—with duties which have to do with divine things'.

The families of ministers ought to be examples of good to all other families, although this can be very challenging. Ministers should take heed of pride; it is a sin that turned angels into devils. He must be of good repute among his neighbours, and under no reproach from his former life. To encourage all faithful ministers, we have Christ's gracious word of promise, 'Lo, I am with you always, even unto the end of the world' (Matthew 28:20). And He will fit His ministers for their work, and carry them through difficulties with comfort, and reward their faithfulness. But this is not automatic, it requires obedient to the calling, and to make the necessary adjustments in order to be a servant of Christ who takes his family's responsibilities serious alongside other commitments.

6.5 Worshipping God at home, in the church, & in the public square

There are many benefits we receive for worshipping God, the creator of the universe. The Lord gave his people this commandment with a promise of blessings: 'Worship the LORD your God and his blessings will be on your food and water. I will take away sickness from among you, and none will miscarry or be barren in your land. I will give you a full life span. I will send my terror ahead of you and throw into confusion every nation you encounter. I will make all your enemies turn their backs and run' (Exodus 23:25-27). When we make the worship of God a priority, He blesses our food, water; He takes sickness from us, and gives as a full life span; He fights our enemies for us. On the other hand, we may receive God's wrath if we refuse to worship to Him: 'Then I saw another angel flying in midair, and he had the eternal gospel to proclaim to those who live on the earth—to every nation, tribe, language and people. He said in a loud voice, Fear God and give Him glory, because the hour of His judgment has come. Worship him who made the heavens, the earth, the sea and the springs of water (Revelation 14:6-7). All those who will refuse to worship the true God will be judged by the Lord.

In this New Testament times, we can worship God anywhere, and at anytime because God is Spirit and His worshippers must worship Him in Spirit and in truth (John 4:23-24). Some people are of the opinion that God should be worshipped in the church and that people who do not go to church are not pleasing God. Others too are of the opinion that it is enough to pray to God privately, at home; going to church is not really important to such people. The third category of people are of the opinion that doing acts of charity which can be considered as public worship of God is all that is important; going to church or private devotion to God is not really important. The aim of this section is to discuss all these three views in a way that will be helpful to you regarding your personal walk with God and your life in general. Let us define what worship is before we continue our discussion.

Some people define worship as the act of singing slow quiet songs to God. Praises on the other hand, then becomes singing songs with fast tempo to God. Worship and praises are not mere acts of singing. Worship is a general term usually used to describe our obedience to God in relationship to who He is and what He has done for us. In order words, worship means doing things for God and for others just as God has commanded us to do. Worship is our obedience to God; doing what pleases God. If worship is doing what please God, then doing anything outside the will of God can be called idol worship. Idol worship is the same as idolatry. The definition of idolatry, according to Webster, is 'the worship of idols or excessive devotion to, or reverence for some person or thing'. An idol is anything that replaces the one, true God. The most prevalent form of idolatry in Bible times was the worship of images that were thought to embody the various pagan deities (demons). This definition categories idol worship into three: the worship of idols (demons); the worship of 'Self', the worship of the 'World'.

When you give excess devotion to yourself more than God, this can be termed as 'self worship'. This is what the word of God says concerning the days we live in: 'But mark this: There will be terrible times in the last days. People will be lovers of themselves, lovers of money, boastful, proud, abusive, disobedient to their parents, ungrateful, unholy, without love, unforgiving, slanderous, without self-control, brutal, not lovers of the good, treacherous, rash, conceited, lovers of pleasure rather than lovers of God (2 Timothy 3:1-4). You are an idol worshipper if you love yourself more than God, or if you always do things to please yourself instead of pleasing God.

When you give devotion or reverence to the systems of the world more than what God says, that is worshipping the 'World' (1 John 2:15-17; Luke 15:11-32). The systems of this world are most of the time different from what God says we should do. God's way are the best. The word of God says 'The world and its desires will pass away, but the man who does the will of God lives forever (1 John 2:17). Make obedience to God's commandments a priority if you want to live forever.

As already mentioned, when you give devotion to any of the activities of Satan such is witchcraft, divination, sorceries, talking to dead people, devil worshipping, talking to spirits or demons; these are all idol worship. God warns His people before they entered the Promised Land against such practices as follows: When you enter the land the LORD your God is giving you, do not learn to imitate the detestable ways of the nations there. Let no one be found among you who sacrifices his son or daughter in the fire, who practices divination or sorcery, interprets omens, engages in witchcraft, or casts spells, or who is a medium or spiritist or who consults the dead. Anyone who does these things is detestable to the LORD, and because of these detestable practices the LORD your God will drive out those nations before you. You must be blameless before the LORD your God (Deuteronomy 18:9-13). Many people especially in Western societies do not know that practicing witchcraft or sorcery or magic, talking to dead people or spirits are all abomination to God. Such people will not enter heaven unless the change their ways. Everybody has a duty to worship God; it is the duty of the church to keep on reminding people to worship this Great God.

Coming back to our discussion, the word of God says we must give the appropriate importance to all the three ways and forms of worshipping God: First, Private worship of God is highly encouraged (Luke 5:15-16). But if you worship or pray to God alone at home or privately you may miss a lot of blessings from worshipping God in the congregational context because some blessings can only be received in the church context, when believers meet and do things together to please God (James 4:14-16). The church is an assembly of believers. When believers meet together, a lot of blessings are released from heaven upon them (Matthew 18:20). There are certain knowledge or information that can only be received through a personal contact with God himself; but there are some too that can only be received in a church context. God told Joshua 'Be strong and very courageous. Be careful to obey all the law my servant Moses gave you; do not turn from it to the right or to the left, that you may be successful wherever you go' (Joshua 1:7). God told, Joshua who took over the leadership mantle from Moses, to be courageous and obey all that Moses taught him. God was not going to repeat all that He told Moses to Joshua. A lot of believers will not listen to what their leaders will tell them. They expect God to speak to them direct. Yes, God can speak to you direct and you must desire for Him to speak to you direct, but there are certain things God has already told the church, and He expects you to know these from the church. One of the reasons why many people have questions about the Bible and God is because they have not sat under a man of God in a true word base church to be taught about the things of God.

Now about our public worship of God, if you do not worship God in public sphere, then you are refusing to be a light and a blessing to other people who have not yet come to the light of Christ's glory. Jesus says:' you are the light of the world. A city on a hill cannot be hidden. Neither do people light a lamp and put it under a bowl. Instead they put it on its stand, and it gives light to everyone in the house. In the same way, let your light shine before men, that they may see your good deeds and praise your Father in heaven' (Matthew 5:14-15). Hebrews 13:12-13 says 'And so Jesus also suffered outside the city gate to make the people holy through His own blood. Let us, then, go to him outside the camp, bearing the disgrace He bore'. Our service to God in reaching out to people outside the church with the kingdom blessings can be considered as our public worship of God not just singing or praising God in public places. Believers are called upon to help people who are lost in their sins; the hopeless, the poor, the prodigal sons and daughters of God; these are some of our public acts worship of God. Jesus Christ is our example. The Bible says 'how God anointed Jesus of Nazareth with the Holy Spirit and power, and how he went around doing good and healing all who were under the power of the devil, because God was with him' (Acts 10:38). Sometimes, our public acts worship of God may attract opposition, persecutions, insults, hatred, but we are called to follow the example of Jesus Christ, who endured sufferings for our sake (1 Peter 2:21-25).

As already indicated, private worship is anything we do privately; between us and God; for God and for fellow human beings. Prayer, giving of

> Yet the news about Him spread all the more, so that crowds of people came to hear Him and to be healed of their sicknesses. But Jesus often withdrew to lonely places and prayed (Luke 5:15-16).

offering in the church, giving of alms to the poor, our singing, and clapping are all acts of worship to God.

From this text, we see Jesus spending some time alone praying to the Father. In the same way, everybody must set some time apart to pray to God alone. In simple terms, the word private has to do with personal issues and with God. Private worship is the worship that takes place between you and God alone. We can therefore say that to worship God privately, means to worship God alone. Sitting at home to pray alone, meditation, reading the Bible, and singing to God are all good spiritual exercises. All these can help the believer to grow in their journey of faith. There are at times when you have to be alone, to pray, to meditate, and to seek the face of God alone. Do you want to know God's will for your life? Dr David Jeremiah shared something on the need for people to spend time alone with God in order to hear His will for their lives:

> When people tell me they are having difficulty discerning God's will for their life, I want to ask one question: How much quiet, still time are you spending in God's presence, listening to Him through prayer and His Word? I do not believe God wants us to be confused about His will and calling for our life. But I also believe that God is not interested in competing with the roar of our culture in order to get our attention and be heard. If we spend more time listening to the voices all around us—musicians, celebrities, commentators, friends, and yes, preachers—than we spend listening to Him, it's no surprise that we are often confused." –David Jeremiah

I think this is a very good advice, especially for people who are in the habit of looking for answers to their problems from people other than from God. Do you want to hear from God? How much quiet time are you spending in God's presence, listening to Him through prayer and His Word? Learn to wait on the Lord so that when he speaks to you, you can hear his voice.

Meditation is one of the most effective methods for an individual to reach a higher state of self-awareness. Meditation takes the mind beyond the distractions and of the moment to a broader level of awareness that notices the causes and patterns in events. For example, in meditative state, I can get beyond my anger to become aware that I am angry, and then reach a stage of reflection or insight as to its causes. This can help me to calm down, and to decide which course of action is appropriate to take in order to bring about peace.

Private Prayer and open prayer: There are at times when you will have to pray alone. And there are at times when you will have to pray openly with other people. Both forms of prayers are necessary. What matters is your attitude towards each form of prayer, and when to engage in each of them. Private prayer to God is encouraged by Jesus Christ himself:

> And when you pray, do not be like the hypocrites, for they love to pray standing in the synagogues and on the street corners to be seen by men. I tell you the truth; they have received their reward in full. But when you pray, go into your room, close the door and pray to your Father, who is unseen. Then your Father, Who sees what is done in secret, will reward you (Matthew 6:5-6).

Some people go to church, to offer prayers and they do this so as to attract notice, the worshipper standing apart as if absorbed in prayer, while secretly glancing round to watch the impression which he might be making on others who were looking on. And so, Jesus condemns such attitude towards prayer. But the fact that some people misconduct themselves in such a manner regarding open prayers does not mean open corporate prayers in the church environment with other believers is not a good thing. It is expected that believers come together to prayer together. if fact there are many benefits of cooperate prayers. There are moments when praying alone becomes a challenge; praying with other people can help your spirituality a lot. Let us look at this example in the Bible:

> On their release, Peter and John went back to their own people and reported all that the chief priests and elders had said to them. When they heard this, they

> raised their voices together in prayer to God... After they prayed, the place where they were meeting was shaken. And they were all filled with the Holy Spirit and spoke the word of God boldly (Acts 4:23-31).

Here, we see cooperate open prayer at work, where all the believers came together to pray for the move of God. The point we have been making in this section is that praying alone is good, and praying with fellow believers is also good; learn to balance the two. Let us discuss the subject of fasting in the next section.

Private Fasting and open fasting:

To fast means to abstain from all or some kinds of food or drink, especially as a religious observance. I encourage those with health problems to consult a qualified medical practitioner before fasting. Fasting is a means of getting our minds back on the reality that we are not self-sufficient. Fasting is very good. It helps us acknowledge our dependency, especially on God. We must fast to get clear answers from God about our daily routines and in particular, issues that concerns our lives here and hereafter. The Bible records that great men of faith such as Moses, Elijah, Daniel, Paul and Jesus Himself fasted so that they might draw closer to God. Jesus acknowledged that His true disciples, once He was no longer with them in the flesh, would need to fast to regain and renew their zeal to serve Him (Mark 2:18-20). On fasting, Jesus has this to say:

> When you fast, do not look somber as the hypocrites do, for they disfigure their faces to show men they are fasting. I tell you the truth; they have received their reward in full. But when you fast, put oil on your head and wash your face, so that it will not be obvious to men that you are fasting, but only to your Father, who is unseen; and your Father, who sees what is done in secret, will reward you (Matthew 6:16-17).

they prayed, the place where they were meeting was shaken. And they were all filled with the Holy Spirit and spoke the word of God boldly (Acts 4:23-31).

God is not fooled by appearances. We cannot fake behavior to impress Him. He knows that inside the best of us lurk dark thoughts of hatred, pride, and lust—internal problems only He can deal with. Jesus goes on to present a truly radical way of life, free of pretense in our worship to God. There are also times when you have to fast in the open, with other people, crying to the Lord together.

In the Old Testament times, we see at various times and in various situations the prophets calling on the nations to repent and fast together for the mercies of God. For example, when the Lord sent Jonah to the city of Nineveh to preach repentance there because of the wickedness of the people, the Bible says, 'the Ninevites believed God. They declared a fast, and all of them, from the greatest to the least, put on sackcloth' (Jonah 3:5). This particular example was cooperate open fasting involving every living thing in the city including animals. It is my prayer that God will send a strong warning message to our leaders to lead our nation to repentance.

Private giving and open giving

There are at times when you have to give in secret, and there are at times when you will be required to make a public donation. Let us look at private giving first.

> Be careful not to do your 'acts of righteousness' before men, to be seen by them. If you do, you will have no reward from your Father in heaven. So when you give to the needy, do not announce it with trumpets, as the hypocrites do in the synagogues and on the streets, to be honored by men. I tell you the truth; they have received their reward in full. But when you give to the needy, do not let your left hand know what your right hand is doing, so that your giving may be in secret. Then your Father, who sees what is done in secret, will reward you (Matthew 5:1-4).

When you give to the church or to help the needy, do not announce it; do not tell people what you have done. God is not happy with such attitude. Secondly, you may be tempted to expect a reward from the person you helped. Many people have been hurt by the people they helped because those they helped did not show appreciation. Understandably, it can be a painful experience. This is why God is telling us to expect the reward from Him. Proverbs 19:17 says 'He who is kind to the poor lends to the LORD, and He the LORD will reward him for what he has done'. God will bless you for helping the needy and for sponsoring his kingdom work.

Let us discuss the subject of cooperate giving. There are at times when you will be required to give in a way that other people will know what you have given to the church or for any other charitable purposes. There is nothing wrong to participate in such fundraising either in the church or outside the church. The Bible is full of examples of this kind of financial or material giving:

> All the believers were one in heart and mind. No one claimed that any of his possessions was his own, but they shared everything they had…There were no needy persons among them. For from time to time those who owned lands or houses sold them, brought the money from the sales and put it at the apostles' feet, and it was distributed to anyone as he had need (Acts 4:32-35).

In this very particular case, the church agreed that each member brings what he or she has to the leadership of the church for distribution. The lesson here is that, there are at times when private giving would be required in the same way that open giving will be required at other times. Church members are to follow the instructions their leaders will give them as they are led by the Holy Spirit. If you have been asked by your church leaders to record your offerings and donations in your membership book, go ahead and follow the directives. If for some reason, you cannot follow the instructions of the church, it is better to have an open and frank discussion with the leadership so that you will be exempted. This approach is better than rebelling against the instructions of the church or lying to the church. Many believers are not blessed because of this attitude of rebelling against the church or lying to the church. Acts chapter five tells of the story of Ananias and Sapphira's bad example. In this account, which we will read very soon, some people argued that the couple were not true believers of the faith that is why they lied to the church leaders about the offering. Since the Bible classified them as part of the believing community, it is my personal believe that the couple were believers who unfortunately lied:

> Now a man named Ananias, together with his wife Sapphira, also sold a piece of property. With his wife's full knowledge he kept back part of the money for himself, but brought the rest and put it at the apostles' feet. Then Peter said, "Ananias, how is it that Satan has so filled your heart that you have lied to the Holy Spirit and have kept for yourself some of the money you received for the land? Didn't it belong to you before it was sold? And after it was sold, wasn't (was not) the money at your disposal? What made you think of doing such a thing? You have not lied to men but to God. When Ananias heard this, he fell down and died. And great fear seized all who heard what had happened (Acts 5:1-5).

This man and his wife were severely punished by the Lord because they lied about their financial donation. They did not follow the general practice of the church regarding giving. As Peter makes clear, Ananias and Sapphira were punished not for holding back money but for lying about it. They were misrepresenting themselves spiritually, trying to appear especially pious and generous.

At the very beginning of what we know to be church today, God set a stern standard of absolute honesty and integrity. Please always follow the guidelines your church will give. Obedience is better than sacrifice (1 Samuel 15:22). If for some reason you are not able to follow, please do not pretend you are following the regulations of that church. Honesty is the best policy. But those who obey the Lord's commands will always be blessed.

6.6 Balanced priority in Christian missions

Christian mission is the work the church does outside the church community for people and the society. Mission is in the heart of God. God left heaven and stepped into His world to help us because of our sinful condition. God took the ultimate step towards fellowship with us through His historic visit to this planet in the person of His Son, Jesus Christ.

Christians are also called to step outside the church building and go into the real world to offer service in the name of God to the society. God is telling the church to step into the world to share the kingdom message. This is one of our public acts of worship to God. The kingdom of God is the reign of God in people's life on this earth, and the world to come. Jesus says 'if I drive out demons by the finger of God, then the kingdom of God has come to you' (Luke 11:20). The kingdom of God come upon your life as you read this book.

Missionaries voluntarily sacrifice their lives to reach people especially those in crisis with some kind of help. They sacrifice their lives to take the gospel message to hostile and dangerous communities. In times of disaster, missionaries and relief workers are the first to get to the disaster scene and the last to leave the scene. These are some of the reasons for discussing Christian missions in this book. I would like to encourage you, dear reader to participate in some kind of Christian missionary activities wherever you find yourself. Christian missionary activities are nonviolent, peaceful, and the bringing of the good news of God's kingdom and other humanitarian services to people locally and internationally.

David Livingstone (March 1813 – May 1873), a Scottish Congregationalist who pioneered the medical missionary with the London Missionary Society and an explorer in Africa is an example of the many men and women who worked as missionaries for the betterment of humanity. His missionary travels, 'disappearance' and death in Africa, and subsequent glorification as posthumous national hero in 1874 led to the founding of several major central African Christian missionary initiatives carried forward in the era of the European 'Scramble for Africa'.

There is one truth in different context and one Bible in different languages. In the context of missions, Dr Dana L. Robert, Professor of International missions at Boston University School of Theology, argued that 'evangelism is the heart of mission'. Evangelism which is the announcement or proclamation of the message about the kingdom of God was such a key feature in the ministry of Jesus Christ and so must it be in Christian missions. Evangelism should be the main activity of Christian missions because of the importance of the salvation of the human soul. The chief aim of evangelism is to bring souls to God for eternal life- for people to be saved and to make it to heaven after death. But on the other hand, if the church does not respond to other material and social needs of the society, it is not discharging its full responsibility. Read Matthew 25: 31-46:

> When the Son of Man [Jesus Christ] comes in His glory and all the angels with Him He will sit on his throne in heavenly glory. All the nations will be gathered before Him and He will separate the people one from another as a shepherd separates the sheep from the goats. He will put the sheep on his right and the goats on his left. Then the King will say to those on His right, 'Come, you who are blessed by my Father; take your inheritance, the kingdom prepared for you since the creation of the world. For I was hungry and you gave Me something to eat, I was thirsty and you gave Me something to drink, I was a stranger and you invited Me in I needed clothes and you clothed Me, I was sick and you looked after Me, I was in prison and you came to visit me. Then the righteous will answer Him, 'Lord, when did we see You hungry and feed You, or thirsty and give you something to drink? When did we see You a stranger and invite you in , or needing clothes and clothe You? When did we see You sick or in prison and go to visit You?' The King will reply, 'I tell you the truth, whatever you did for one of the least of these brothers of mine, you did for Me. Then He will say to those on His left, 'Depart from Me you who are cursed, into the eternal fire prepared for the devil and his angels. For I was hungry and you gave Me nothing to eat, I was thirsty and you gave Me nothing to drink, I was a stranger and you did not invite Me in, I needed clothes and you did not clothe Me, I was sick and in prison and you did not look after Me. They also will answer, 'Lord, when did we see You hungry or thirsty or a stranger or needing clothes or sick or in prison, and did not help You?' He will reply, 'I tell you the truth, whatever you did not do for one of the least of these, you did not do for Me. Then they will go away to eternal punishment, but the righteous to eternal life.

Christ Jesus, the soon coming king is not happy whenever someone is in need and we do not do anything about it especially if we are in the position to help. The teachings of that wonderful last days of Christ's ministry, which have occupied so many of our pages, are closed with this tremendous picture of universal judgment. Note the surprises of the judgment. Because of this, this teaching is one to be gazed upon with silent awe, and to respond in repentance if we have not been caring for the needy and the less privilege in our society. A balanced priority is needed in our missionary activities where the needy are cared for, and the gospel of salvation is preached to lost sinners.

The gospel of Jesus Christ can have positive effects on every aspect of the human personality and the society as a whole. Unfortunately some of the people who have been entrusted with the message of salvation have relegated this message to the background of their activities if not abandoned totally and are mainly concerned about the temporary benefits of the gospel message. Benevolent services such as charity work, musical shows, coffee mornings, running of orphanages are very good, but they are not good enough to save the human soul from hell. People can only be saved when they put their faith in Jesus Christ, repent of their sins, be baptized and aim to live a godly life. We need balanced missions activities.

In this book, am proposing a model based on Matthew chapter ten for keeping evangelism at the heart of missions and at the same time respond critically to any crisis or any need in our society. In this account, Jesus sent out his twelve disciples to demonstrate the kind of kingdom He came to establish: a kingdom that has brought us forgiveness, healing, liberation, and the good news. Jesus says, 'As you go, preach this message: 'The kingdom of heaven is near.' Heal the sick, raise the dead, and cleanse those who have leprosy, drive out demons. Freely you have received, freely give' (Matthew 10:7-8). This text enjoins believers to proclaim the kingdom message and at the same time attend to the needs of the people in Christian missions. A similar model may be needed in any situation you may find yourself. How can you keep the most important thing in your life at the heart of your activities and at the same time, spend some time on other activities? A lot of blessings are bestowed on Christians by the Lord Jesus Christ when they meet together with in the church or in small groups. What happens at Christian meetings is the focus of next section discussion.

6.7 Prioritising what happen at Christian gatherings

Many Christians love to worship God through music, church attendance, and offerings but keep neglecting some other aspects of worship which God requires of them. The prophet Amos warned the people of old to keep a balanced priority:

> I hate, I despise your religious feasts; I cannot stand your assemblies. Even though you bring me burnt offerings and grain offerings, I will not accept them. Though you bring choice fellowship offerings, I will have no regard for them. Away with the noise of your songs! I will not listen to the music of your harps. But let justice roll on like a river, righteousness like a never-failing stream! (Amos 5:21-24).

Meeting together is good. Singing to God during worship is good because it is the Lord who commands as to do so. But the people had neglected some aspects of their worship of God- justice to the poor and the alien, and maintaining righteousness. And so God had to rebuke them through the prophet Amos. The lesson here is that every local church must constantly reform the way they do things, and repent when necessary. How is your church doing? Do you agree with your pastor to carry out changes in the church? Which area do you think your local church needs reformation?

Does God care about your church?

If you are tempted to doubt it, look closely at the seven letters Jesus sent to the seven churches in Revelation chapters two and three. The Lord of the universe knew the state of each of these churches and its precise situation. In each letter, Jesus told John who received the divine revelation to write about specific people, places and events. Jesus praised believers for their success and told them how to correct their failures. Just as Jesus cared for each of these churches, He cares for ours too. He wants the church to reach its greatest potential.

When we do not neglect justice, righteousness, and other vital aspects of our worship, then our songs become a joyful song to the Lord, because the psalms for example, were meant to be sung—and shouted: 'Sing to him a new song; play skillfully, and shout for joy' (Psalm 33:3). Singing spiritual songs to God brings down blessings from heaven and singing is good for the soul of the human personality as well. How often do you sing to God?

> Then I looked and heard the voice of many angels, numbering thousands upon thousands, and ten thousand times ten thousand. They encircled the throne and the living creatures and the elders. In a loud voice they sang: "Worthy is the Lamb, who was slain, to receive power and wealth and wisdom and strength and honor and glory and praise!" Then I heard every creature in heaven and on earth and under the earth and on the sea, and all that is in them, singing: "To him who sits on the throne and to the Lamb be praise and honor and glory and power, forever and ever!" The four living creatures said, "Amen," and the elders fell down and worshiped (Revelation 5:11-14).

Even angels, heavenly hosts, and all creation, sing and worship God! How often do you sing to God?

William Booth, the founder of the Salvation Army Church, believing the 19th-century English church had become too refined to reach the cities' poor, took the gospel into the streets. He organized his ministry workers into a 'salvation army' complete with uniforms and military ranks. With hecklers and drunkards abounding, the 'army' did not always find preaching easy or safe. A local builder, Charles William Fry, offered himself and his three sons as bodyguards. As it happened, all four played brass instruments, which they carried along to accompany singing. Booth's rowdier supporters were soon dragging along concertinas, bells, hunting horns, banjos, tambourines, and drums to praise the Lord. One of the leaders said, 'It sounds as if a brass band has gone out of its mind!' Salvation Army recruits did not stick to traditional hymns but invented their own words for rousing popular tunes. Booth said, 'Why *should* the devil have all the best tunes?' Soon 400 bands were crashing about in England, playing hit tunes with Christian words. Let us sing a joyful song to God! Praise the Lord for He is kind. His mercies endure forever.

The best music available to the Great God

King David and his people would have liked that spirit. Many of the psalms were meant to be sung, and sung joyfully. Modern church formality seems far removed from their frequent command:

'Sing for joy! Shout aloud!' Their instruments included cymbals, tambourines, trumpets, ram's horns, harps, and lyres, sometimes dancing erupted. The world, in the psalmist's imagination, cannot contain the delight God inspires. A new song must be sung. 'Shout for joy to the LORD, all the earth, burst into jubilant song' says Psalm 98:4. But all these church activities must be properly balanced; else the Lord will say, 'away with the noise of your songs! I will not listen to the music of your harps. But let justice roll on like a river, righteousness like a never-failing stream! (Amos 5:21-24).

6.8 Being born again requires that you shift your priorities.

When one becomes a child of God through faith in Jesus Christ 'the old lifestyle is gone the new has come' says the apostle Paul in 2 Corinthian 5:17. The new believer must now spend more of his or her time on the things of God such as prayers, reading the Bible, church attendance, fasting, working hard to feed the family, giving alms to the poor and so on. These are all spiritual activities to help you grow as a new born 'spiritual baby' (1 Peter 2:2). Being born again requires that you shift your priorities. What about old friends and acquaintances? If your friendship with your old friends will not help you to grow in your new faith, then it is a wise thing to stay away from them until you are in the position to witness Christ to them. The word of God gives this advice:

> Do not be yoked together with unbelievers. For what do righteousness and wickedness have in common? Or what fellowship can light have with darkness? What harmony is there between Christ and Belial ? What does a believer have in common with an unbeliever? What agreement is there between the temple of God and idols? For we are the temple of the living God. As God has said: "I will live with them and walk among them, and I will be their God, and they will be my people. Therefore come out from them and be separate, says the Lord. Touch no unclean thing, and I will receive you. I will be a Father to you, and you will be my sons and daughters, says the Lord Almighty. Since we have these promises, dear friends, let us purify ourselves from everything that contaminates our body and spirit, perfecting holiness out of reverence for God.

A yoke is a curved wooden bar that fits across the necks of two animals used to pull a plow or wagon. Yoke together a short, speedy calf with a tall, sluggish ox, and you are asking for trouble. Paul probably had in mind the false teachers who so often bedeviled the Corinthians, but his wise principle applies to many other alliances between believers and unbelievers. Do you know that an unbeliever can easily put a believer friend in trouble?' 'Do not be misled: "Bad company corrupts good character' (1 Corinthians 15:33).

In the context of marriage, if a believer is going to get married, the advice is that the believer must look for a fellow believer to marry. But if a believer has an unbelieving husband or wife, the believer should not divorce him or her. The unbelieving partner has been sanctified, (set apart for salvation) by the believing partner (see 2 Corinthians 7:12-16).
The fatal effects of neglecting Scriptural precepts for marriages clearly appear. Instead of a help mate, sometimes a marriage which is between a believer and unbeliever can be a snare. Those whose cross is to be unequally united, without their wilful fault, may expect consolation under it. But when a believer contracts such a union against the express warnings of God, they must expect much distress, although the Lord will still be with them.

The caution also extends to common conversation. We should not join in friendship with wicked men and unbelievers unless we are influencing them positively. Though we cannot wholly avoid seeing and hearing, and being with such, yet we should never choose them for friends. We must not defile ourselves by conversing with those who defile themselves with sin. Come out from the workers of iniquity, and be separated from their vain and sinful pleasures and conformity to the corruptions of this present evil world. If it is an enviable privilege to be a child of an earthly king, how much more is the dignity and happiness we will derive for being children of the Almighty God?

In conclusion, there is a season — a certain time appointed by God for its being and continuance, which no human wisdom or providence can alter. Therefore every season requires a certain lifestyle and activities which means, your priorities should be shifting depending on the season you find yourself.

Know the season you are in and begin to set your priorities right. This may even require a complete change of lifestyle. Paul says 'When I was a child, I talked like a child; I thought like a child, I reasoned like a child. When I became a man, I put the ways of childhood behind me (1 Corinthians 3:11). Times of transition are strenuous, but I love them. They are opportunities to purge, rethink priorities, and be intentional about new habits. To change priorities can be a very challenging task, but the reward as we have noted in this book is good.

Matthew Henry's Concise Commentary on Ecclesiastes 3:1-10 says: 'To expect unchanging happiness in a changing world must end in disappointment. To bring ourselves to our state in life is our duty and wisdom in this world. God's whole plan for the government of the world will be found altogether wise, just, and good. Then let us seize the favourable opportunity for every good purpose and work. The time to die is fast approaching. Thus labour and sorrow fill the world. This is given to us so that we may always have something to do; none were sent into the world to be idle'.

In this book and in this chapter in particular, we have discussed at various examples of balanced priorities. It is hoped that you will apply the principles discussed in this book for the betterment of your life, others and the wider society.

> Now all has been heard; here is the conclusion of the matter: Fear God and keep his commandment, for this is the whole duty of man. For God will bring every deed into judgment, including every hidden thing, whether it is good or evil (Ecclesiastes 12:13-14).

GOD RICHLY BLESSED YOU!

Consulting Books

Berger, P. (1999). *The Desecularization of the Worl: Resurgent Religion and World Politics.* Michigan: Ethics and Public Centre and Wm. B. Eerdmans Publishing Co.

Heelas, P. &. Woodhead, L. (2005). *The Spiritual Revolution: Why Religion is giving way to Spirituality.* Oxford: Blackwell Publishing Ltd.

International Bible Society, (eds.) (2005) The Bible: *New International Version,* London: Hodder & Stoughton.

Robert, D., Gunter, W. and Oduyoye, M. (1997). *Evangelism as the heart of mission.* New York: General Board of Global Ministries, the United Methodist Church.

Sheldrake, P. (2013). *A brief history of spirituality.* Hoboken: John Wiley & Sons.

Shelley, B. & Shelley, B. (1993). *Theology for ordinary people.* Downers Grove, Ill.: InterVarsity Press.

Williams, R. (2014). *Being Christian.* London: Spckpublishing

Williams, R., (2012). *Faith in the Public Square,* London: Bloomsbury.

Yogananda, Walters, J. and Yogananda, (2003). *God is for everyone.* Nevada City, Calif.: Crystal Clarity Publishers.

Zohar, D. & Marshall, I. (2004). *Spiritual capital.* London: Bloomsbury.